71 10782   BENTLEY, J.   629.2292

Old Time Steam Cars.

Oldtime Steam Cars

by John Bentley

New York

Published by Arco Publishing Company, Inc., 219 Park Avenue South, New York, N.Y. 10003.
Second Printing, 1969.
Copyright 1953 by Fawcett Publications Inc.
Standard Book Number 668-02073-3
Library of Congress Catalog Card Number: 53-4010

Printed in U.S.A.

Contents

INTRODUCTION 3
THE STEAM CAR STORY 6
THE STANLEY 26
THE WHITE 46
THE LOCOMOBILE 56
THE STEAM CAR ALBUM . . . 59

American 60
American-Waltham 62
Amoskeag 63
Baker 64
Binney & Burnham 66
Boss 67
Brecht 68
Brooks 69
Capitol 70
Century 71
Clark 72
Cloughley 73
Coats 74
Coldwell 75
Conrad 75
Cotta 76
Coulthard 76
Covert 77
Crouch 78
Curran 79
Dawson 80
Delling 80

Detroit 82
Doble 83
Doble-Detroit 88
Eclipse 89
Elite 90
Empire 90
Foster 91
Gearless 92
Geneva 94
Grout 95
Steam Car Geography . . . 99
Production Span 99
Halsey 100
Hoffman 101
Hood 102
Howard 103
Hudson 103
Jaxon 104
Jenkins 104
Johnson 105
Kensington 106
Kidder 107
Lane 108
Leach 110
Marlboro 110
Maryland 111
McDonald 112
Meteor 112
Milwaukee 113
Mobile 114

Moncrief 118
Morgan 118
Morse 119
National 120
Neustadt-Perry 120
New England 121
New York 122
Porter 122
Prescott 123
Puritan 124
Reading 124
Richmond 125
Rochester 126
Ross 127
Scott-Newcomb 128
Skene 130
Steamobile 131
Stearns 132
Sterling 134
Sunset 135
Sweany 135
Toledo 136
Tractobile 138
Twombly 139
Victor 140
Westfield 142
G. E. Whitney 142
R. S. Whitney 143
Wood 144
Wood Loco 144

Building Up Steam
An Introduction by the Author

THOUGH I YIELD TO NO ONE in my admiration for that brilliantly ingenious but absurdly complicated and sadly inefficient piece of machinery —the internal combustion engine, I must admit that some intensive research into the history of the steam car stopped me cold. Time and again that sixty-four dollar question popped up in stentorian tones, clamoring for an answer: "Why was the steam car a failure?"

Most of us have long since "accepted" the gasoline automobile (together with its enormous commercial ramifications) as part of our daily lives. When a steam car enthusiast, crying in the wilderness, reminds us that the superior steam engine was commercially defeated after a brief and bitter battle with the inferior internal combustion engine, we nod indifferently. Yet consider this: given freedom of choice during an era when the modern manufacturing giants of the automotive industry were scarcely born, the public yet took to a crude gasoline machine depending on explosions and not even in the same league with its steam rival, no matter what the score.

Ridiculous, isn't it?

Here is what US Motor of July 1926 said in an article reviewing the Delling Steam Car: "It is reasonably certain that if even a fraction of the many millions spent in the development of the gasoline car had been spent on steam car development, there would be several successful steam cars on the market today."

This masterly understatement, tempered down for commercial reasons, should have been re-worded to conclude: " . . . there would not be a single gasoline car on the market today."

At best, the thermal efficiency of the internal combustion engine may reach 35 per cent, whereas that of the steam engine tops 90 per cent. This means that only a small proportion of every gallon of gas you buy does any actual work in propelling your automobile; the bulk of that gallon, instead of being converted into valuable energy is transformed into useless heat that calls for a complex and power-consuming cooling system to get rid of it!

Next, the low-speed torque (hauling power) even of the multi-cylinder gas engine is pitifully poor; and for this reason it became necessary first to evolve sliding gear and synchromesh transmissions, and later—by way of "improvement"—various expensive, complicated and heavy torque converters which compensate (to some extent) for this shortcoming by transforming speed into energy and vice versa, as the occasion demands.

A two-cylinder, double action steam engine with less than 40 moving parts, provides as many power impulses per crankshaft revolution as an *eight-cylinder* "explosion" engine cluttered-up with a mass of bewildering gadgets; and it requires neither clutch nor torque converter of any kind. You can gear it direct to the axle of your car.

Place a modern automobile with its front bumper against a wall, then start it up, select low gear and let in the clutch. What happens? The engine stalls immediately. Do the same with a steam car and the engine will continue to spin the rear wheels until the tires blow up!

In assessing the efficiency of today's automobile—particularly where this refers to sports or racing cars—two highly desirable criteria usually come to mind. The first is the magic figure of 300 bhp per ton weight, and this (with an unsupercharged engine) is achieved in rare instances as yet. The second is an output of 100 bhp per liter (61 cu. in.) displacement, not so far attained by any normally aspirating internal combustion engine.

With a properly designed steam unit, neither of these objectives would present any difficulty; indeed, back in 1906, Fred Marriott's Florida Stanley Racer, a so-called "freak" which set a new world's record at 127.66 mph, came pretty close to these ideals. It developed 250 bhp for a weight of less than 2,200 pounds and a displacement of 206 cu. in. That, remember, was 48 years ago! Nor did this machine require umpteen cylinders, overhead camshafts, trains of driving gears, multiple carburetors and a tricky ignition system involving costly spark plugs with a useful working life of, perhaps, an hour or two.

As to everyday motoring needs, be it in terms of pick-up, flexibility, speed, reliability, running economy, silence or low upkeep costs, a modern steam car could make a monkey out of the conventional internal combustion automobile under any conditions. Furthermore, it could be manufactured and sold in quantities for about half the price of your present car—excellent value as that may be.

There is only one drawback to the steamer, if indeed it can be called a drawback. To raise a full head of steam from dead cold, even with a perfected flash boiler, probably would take a couple of minutes. This is no longer than required to give your gasoline engine a chance to warm-up to efficient working temperature before leaving home; yet the average owner wouldn't see it that way. An hour wasted in a Sunday afternoon traffic jam is quite in order, but two minutes to get started each morning would seem like an intolerable squandering of valuable time!

This strange impatience which is the peculiar quirk of the motorist, who for some reason always has been in a hurry and always has expected everything to happen immediately, if not sooner, is probably what defeated the steam car. Had the flash boiler, electrically fired by the turn of an ignition key, been perfected before the self-starter, the chances are that the steamer would have won out; but when Cadillac pioneered that valuable adjunct as standard equipment in 1912, ridding motorists of the bugbear of cranking their gasoline engines by hand at the risk of broken bones, it still took a steamer five or ten minutes to get going from cold. And that was too long. Progress in metallurgy and thermo-dynamics, it seems, reached the required point a decade too late to save the steam car.

It is claimed that at various times some 125 or more makes of steam cars came and went on the American market. In support of this, lists of names have been published, supposedly indicating these makes; but careful research into contemporary periodicals reveals a different story. In many cases, what appear to be the names of two or three different vehicles turn out to be one and the same machine.

Again, several names of supposed steamers turned out to belong to gasoline autos shrouded in contemporary obscurity, their identity further obliterated by the passing of years. This is true of such makes as Gaeth, Keystone,

Randolph and several others blithely tossed into the steam car potage, and the situation is further complicated by a number of manufacturers who started building steam cars, saw the writing on the wall and switched to gasoline vehicles, or worked both sides of the street at the same time. The Century, Cloughley, Conrad, Grout, Hoffman (later Royal Tourist), Jackson, Locomobile, Maryland, Morse and Sunset steamers all come under this category. Here and there a firm played it win, place and show by simultaneously offering a choice of steam, gasoline or electric cars—a case in point being the Kensington.

Most inaccurate and confusing of all are the assumed dates of inception of many steam cars and their "estimated" life span. Where much of this chronology comes from is a mystery all the more perplexing because it has little bearing on fact.

To secure a reasonably accurate fund of contemporary information on the 84 makes of steamers reviewed in the Album, involved an intensive study of nearly 500 publications. Even then, determining the chronology of some of these vehicles called for a process of deductive research and careful elimination via endless cross-references.

That there were others besides the 84 manufacturers catalogued in this book is not in doubt; but to secure authentic data about them is another matter. Several times, some tantalizing reference to a name cropped up in an article and started a chase after information that ended in a blind alley. And since the inclusion of these phantom steamers would contribute nothing to the informative value of the present book, they have purposely been left out. Even so, I would guess that (allowing for these imaginative duplications of names) about 100 makes is nearer the real total.

A brief study of the longevity of steamers is, perhaps, also worth recording. Some 42 makes lasted only one or two years; 11 manufacturers survived three and four years respectively; seven kept going for five years; two for six years and two more for a decade each. The longest lived bona fide concern, strangely enough, was not the famous Stanley enterprise, but the Manchester Locomotive Works which built the Amoskeag Steam Fire Engine from 1867 to 1906—a period of 40 years.

As to the possible future of steam cars, this offers much interesting ground for speculation. That they may come back and eventually supplant the internal combustion automobile is more likely than any casual prophecy might lead us to believe; but for this event we may have to wait until the industrial application of atomic power is an established fact. If it becomes practicable to build miniature "lightweight" atomic piles cooled by water (on the same principle as the Navy's projected Atomic Steam Submarine), the return of the road steamer can be counted on as almost a certainty, for it will not then depend upon any of the present-day liquid fuels but will enjoy the advantage of a practically inexhaustible means of generating steam. But as things stand, there are too many powerful influences and huge financial interests at stake to encourage, or even permit the reappearance of a steam car on a commercial scale.

Kerosene is entirely suitable for producing super-heated steam. Where would the popular use of this fuel leave the vast petroleum corporations with countless millions invested in refineries for producing high-octane gasoline? To these enterprises, kerosene is merely a by-product of no great value, sold far below the cost of gasoline and in far smaller quantities.

Again, with the billion-dollar automotive corporations that are the backbone of the nation's third largest industry, there are numerous subsidiaries engaged in producing "accessories" such as spark plugs, carburetors, ignition systems, transmissions, camshafts, valve springs and what-have-you, most of them not of the slightest use in a steam car. To these firms, the resurgence of the steamer on a big scale would spell ruin and disaster.

From this you may draw your own conclusions. ●

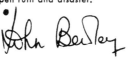

Experimentation by isolated individuals all add up to a formidible case for the steam car, a source of pride and power.

IT SEEMS PROBABLE that the very first steam car (i.e. horseless vehicle propelled by a steam engine) able to move under its own power can be credited to a Jesuit missionary in China about the year 1655. His name was Father Verbiest and his undoubted scientific talents earned him recognition far beyond the ecclesiastical field, for he was not only Astronomer Royal in Pekin, but also Superintendent of the Cannon Foundries during the reign of Emperor Shun Chih of the Ch'ing dynasty.

Father Verbiest performed a number of experiments in steam propulsion before he came up with a practical answer in the form of a small four-wheel carriage with a light body, scaled down for use mainly indoors. Motive power, however, was not original; it consisted of an Aeolipile—a primitive form of steam reaction turbine first described by Hero of Alexandria in his "Pneumatica" (130 BC), but not put into practical use until 1629, when an improved version was built by Giovanni Branca, an Italian chemist. Branca's Aeolipile was a kind of steam windmill with a boiler cast in the shape of a man's head and shoulders. This was filled with water and heated until a jet of steam issued from the mouth and played directly on a paddle wheel. Branca made use of the rotary motion thus obtained to pound drugs, but Father Verbiest saw other possibilities. His version of the Aeolipile, heated by a pan of burning coals, directed its steam jet onto a wheel equipped with four vanes. In turn, this wheel was geared to the wheels of the car which moved at "a good speed" so long as the steam lasted, and could readily be steered.

In about 1680—a quarter of a century after Father Verbiest—Sir Isaac Newton, the great English physicist, designed a steam carriage which logically took this idea a step further. The boiler had an escape pipe pointing backward and the vehicle was propelled directly by reaction from the escaping steam, on the same principle as the modern jet plane.

Newton's drawings showed his steam car to be a crude enough machine, somewhat resembling a Merlin's chair—a wheeled conveyance for invalids named after a

French mathematical instrument manufacturer who came to London. A furnace was provided for the boiler and a seat for the driver, but there does not seem to be any evidence that this vehicle ever actually ran. Yet to this day Newton is often wrongly credited with having pioneered the propulsion of vehicles by the reaction of a steam jet. This, no doubt, is due to the fact that he discovered and formulated the law stating that "every action has an equal and opposite reaction."

Over 80 years elapsed, and the world had to emerge from the dark superstition of the Middle Ages before the next trail-blazer made his appearance in the field of steam propulsion. It was in 1763—during the last decade of the troubled reign of Louis XV of France—that Captain Nicholas Joseph Cugnot designed and ran a steam car built

The Aeolipile, right, a primitive steam turbine conceived in 130 BC was used by Father Verbiest in 1655 in first steam car.

Captain Joseph Nicholas Cugnot's Steam Artillery Tractor of 1763 was France's first horseless carriage. It was never exploited.

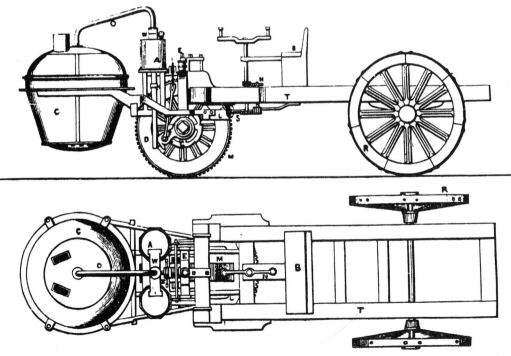

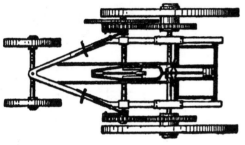

First motorcar specifically designed to carry paying passengers and the first to make 10 mph was William Trevithick's Steam Carriage, 1801.

THE STEAM CAR STORY:

CHRONOLOGY

Father Verbiest's Aeolipile Steam Car 1655
Sir Isaac Newton's Steam Carriage 1680
Capt. Nicholas Cugnot's Artillery Tractor 1763
Dr. Erasmus Darwin's Rotary Motion Steamer 1765
James Watt's Steam Carriage 1769
William Murdock's "Locomotive" 1784
Nathan Read's Tubular Boiler 1790
William Trevithick's Steam Carriage 1801
Oliver Evans' "Orukter Amphibolos" 1805
Dumbell's Flash-Type Generator 1808
Julius Griffith's Steam Carriage 1821
Burstall and Hill's Steam Carriage 1824
Nevill's Oscillating Cylinder Carriage 1825
James and Anderson's Steam Coach 1829
Summers and Ogle's Multi-Tubular Boiler 1830
Sir Goldsworthy Gurney's Steam Coach 1831
Surrey's Steam Tractor 1831
William Hancock's "Autopsy" 1833
Dr. Church's Steam Coach 1833
John Scott Russell's Steam Car 1834
Thomas Rickett's Road Steamer 1858
Richard Dudgeon's Steam Wagon 1860
Dr. J. N. Carhart's Steam Buggy 1871
Ransom E. Old's Steamer 1887
Stephen Roper's Steam Bicycle 1894
Frank Vanell's Steam Carriage 1895
John Einig's Steam Carriage 1896
A. T. Cross' Steam Carriage 1897

to his specifications at the Royal Arsenal in Paris. Cugnot's sponsor was the Duke de Choiseul, minister of war, whose interest stemmed from the fact that this machine was intended to serve as a gun carriage and artillery tractor. Undoubtedly, Cugnot fashioned not only the first steam car built for a specific purpose, but also the prototype of all power-driven army vehicles. On its first run, Cugnot's machine carried four people at 2¾ mph and showed much promise as it chugged through its trials over the cobbled streets of Paris, even though it was a rough, lumbering machine mounted on three wooden wheels with iron tires that supported a gross weight of five tons. The single front wheel, four feet in diameter, provided traction, being driven direct by a two-cylinder engine cast from brass which operated on the single-acting principle; that is, it took in steam and gave out power in only one direction of the stroke. Each cylinder had a bore of 13-in. and derived steam from a huge copper boiler slung well out over the front wheel—presumably to balance the weight of a cannon supported by the two rear wheels. This, however, never was mounted and the "payload" was restricted to passengers.

In 1770, Cugnot built a second steam carriage of improved design which could travel 12 to 15 minutes before stopping to generate fresh steam. It made use of the rack and pinion steering principle common to many of today's fast sports cars, and, had not the Duke de Choiseul gone into exile shortly afterward, there isn't much doubt that Cugnot's vehicle might eventu-

Crude and quaint, Oliver Evans' high sounding "Orukter Amphibolos" steamed 1½ miles in 1805. This was America's first pioneer steam vehicle.

ally have saved Royalist France. But history was to be written differently. During the second trials, the enterprising Cugnot coaxed three mph out of his creaking monster and attempted too sharp a turn at that speed, with the result that the machine capsized.

Paris police reacted unpleasantly by impounding the vehicle to keep it "out of mischief," and by throwing Cugnot (who no longer had a sponsor) in jail to keep him quiet. This was strangely fickle behavior condoned by a War Ministry which had financed the experiments at great expense; but the authorities relented to the extent of allowing the inventor to go into exile, where he remained until after Louis XVI had been beheaded and the Revolution was over. Recalled and pensioned by Napoleon Bonaparte, Cugnot—whose machine had been stored in the Arsenal during all these years without exciting the least interest—was encouraged to renew experiments; but not along the lines of a military vehicle. Napoleon thus lost the chance to endow his artillery with a unique form of mobility, though Cugnot's machine has been preserved to this day.

Two years after Cugnot's original steam carriage (in 1765) Dr. Erasmus Darwin, grandfather of the great and controversial Charles Darwin, laid down some remarkable specifications for a steam carriage. Dr. Darwin was a physician in Lichfield, England, who traveled about the countryside, visiting patients in a horse-drawn sulky laden with books, food and medicine. But as he rode, the good doctor's mind indulged in some interesting flights of imagination

Oliver Evans, engineer and inventor, made many industrial contributions between 1792 and 1811.

This Drop-Valve steam engine, below, was designed by Oliver Evans for use in his Amphibious Digger. It had power enough to haul more than 17 tons. Note flywheel and gears to paddle wheel.

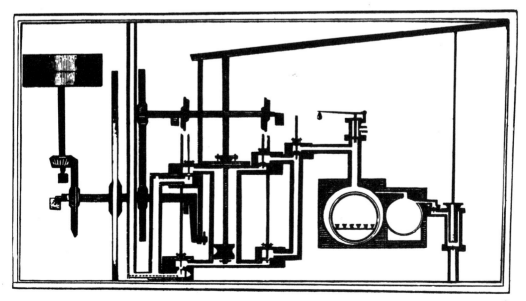

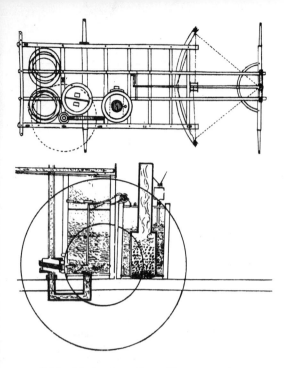

Original design for a Steam Wagon was drawn up by Oliver Evans in 1801. Road wheel was geared to a vertical engine-driven shaft (top). The machine also featured a horizontal flywheel 5 ft. in diameter and a unit-built fire grate boiler.

which ran all the way from poetry to engineering. Some of them envisioned the future so closely they could be called prophetic.

His thoughts concerning a steam-powered vehicle, for instance, he set down as follows:

1. It must have rotary motion.
2. It must be capable of easily altering its direction in any other direction.
3. It should be accelerated, retarded, destroyed (stopped), revived (started) instantly and easily.
4. The bulk weight and expense of the machine to be as small as possible in proportion to the weight.

Every one of these attributes would be required in the successful steam car of today. Indeed, they conform with the characteristics of the modern internal combustion automobile.

As to poetry, one of Dr. Darwin's compositions began thus:

Soon shall they arm unconquered steam afar,
Drag the slow barge, or drive the rapid car;
On far wide waving wings expanded bear
The Flying Chariot through the fields of air . . .

Strangely accurate was the prophecy

made in the last two lines, for on April 20, 1933—a century and a half after they had been written—a steam powered airplane took off from San Francisco Bay Airdrome and made a successful pioneer flight at an average of 100 mph. It was equipped with a 90 hp, two-cylinder steam engine and the crew consisted of George and William Besler, well known in the field of steam propulsion.

Contemporary with Dr. Erasmus Darwin, dreamer, was the great James Watt, an intensely practical inventor even though he suffered from peculiar forms of bias. By 1769, only four years after the good physician had verbally explored the possibilities of steam for motive power, Watt's steam engine was developed to a point where it employed practically all the principles of the modern double-acting, condensing steam engine. Yet James Watt never built a steam carriage and, indeed, viewed the project with strong disfavor. The extremes to which the canny Scotsman was prepared to resort in order to prevent steam power from being harnessed to a road vehicle are puzzling, to say the least. Writing to Dr. Small, a friend of his, concerning a project of this kind in which a linen draper named Moore was deeply interested, Watt remarked: "If Moore does not use my engine to drive his chaises, he can't drive them by steam. If he does, I will stop him!"

Apparently, Watt had no faith in the possibility of steam locomotion on such roads as then existed, but in spite of this he seemed anxious to prevent anyone else from even attempting the idea. It is curious to observe the extremes to which his attitude prompted him. In a patent dated 1784, Watt included a description of a steam carriage which he admitted was very defective. Correspondence concerning this patent with his business partner, Boulton, revealed the following statement: "It can only serve to keep other people from similar patents."

In theory, Watt's patent was very ingenious; it related to the application of a condenser to a steam engine. This condenser was exposed to the wind and cooled either by bellows or a fan. The inventor also sketched out a variable speed gear train consisting of loose gears with an interlocking clutch—a principle much later used in all the "variable selective" transmissions of gasoline cars until the advent of synchro-mesh.

As to materials, however, Watt's steam vehicle certainly was susceptible to improvement. The boiler was to be made of *wood*, or of "thin metal surrounded by

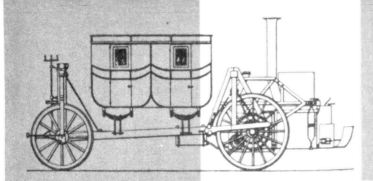

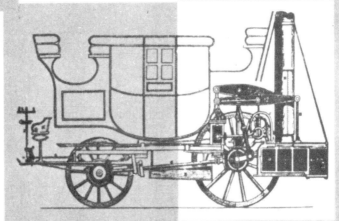

Griffith's picturesque Steam Carriage, above, designed to carry an ambitious load of three tons, was completed in 1822 by Bramah, a famous contemporary engineer and locksmith. It developed boiler trouble. Four wheel drive was a feature of the Burstall and Hill Steam Carriage, right. Scaling six tons, it featured a flash-type boiler and made up to four mph. This, however, was not fast enough.

strengthening hoops and preferably of cylindrical or globular form, with a furnace inside, surrounded by water." Engine specifications called for a double-acting power unit, "either non-condensing, or condensing by means of an air-cooled surface condenser." Two-speed gearing also was included, and the vertical engine was to drive the axle by means of rack and pinion.

Later, Watt decided on copper for the boiler material and coke for fuel. "The shaking of the carriage," he thought, "would supersede the necessity of poking the fire."

Watt's Steam Road Vehicle never was actually built, but it seems likely that his thoughts in this direction were inspired by his assistant, William Murdock, who, despite the disapproval of the boss, had already begun experiments along these lines.

Some 15 years went by before Murdock's ideas finally took the shape of a working steam carriage that worked only too well. How much incentive Murdock derived from his association with the firm of Boulton and Watt is anybody's guess, but in 1784 we find him busily testing out the fruits of his labor down in Cornwall—his native

county—where he was employed at a local tin mine. Beyond doubt, Murdock not only was responsible for the first steam "locomotive" built in England, but must also be given credit for being the first to apply the principle of high pressure steam to a horseless carriage.

The body of his machine consisted of a flat board mounted on three wheels, with the engine and a rectangular copper boiler mounted at the rear. The boiler featured an inclined flue and was heated by a spirit lamp, steam being supplied to a single-cylinder engine with a 3/4-in. bore, placed inside the boiler and of what would be called today "unit construction." The engine's piston rod was coupled to a rocking beam from which a connecting rod descended to the cranked axle driving the twin rear wheels. One of these wheels was "loosely secured" to allow the vehicle to turn, while the front wheel was mounted on a swivel to permit steering. In one respect, however, Murdock was not original: his method of converting the reciprocating motion of a steam engine into the required rotary motion was borrowed from a principle patented by Pickard in 1780.

That Murdock's Steam Carriage (actually a scaled down model) was a going concern is attested to by an amusing interlude during which the vicar of the local parish got the fright of his life. It seems that one evening, returning from his duties at one of the Cornish mines, Murdock decided to test his machine on a level stretch about a mile from town and situated near the parish church. By the time he got the boiler fired up and everything ready it was dark, and to add to complications the vehicle generated steam before Murdock could climb aboard and get matters under control. With startling suddenness the little steam carriage took off by itself and gathered speed down the road. The worthy vicar, happening by at this time, mistook the hissing, fiery monster for the Devil himself, spitting sparks at the darkened landscape! The inventor, needless to say, had a lot of explaining to do.

By this time, interest in steam propulsive machinery had assumed so much importance that it was reaching out beyond the confines of the Old World, across the oceans and into the young and eager continent of America. For instance, the vertical tubular boiler widely used on steam vehicles early this century, was the invention of Nathan Read, a Massachusetts engineer who conceived the idea of a steam carriage in 1788-89. As with nearly all inventors, Read's path was strewn with obstacles and disappointments. His first patent application to Congress fell through, but he went ahead anyway and in 1790 completed a model of a steam carriage equipped with his boiler and featuring another interesting detail. Provision was made for four exhaust pipes pointing backward to help propel the car by steam reaction along the lines of the jet principle.

Read's multi-tubular boiler was a vital step in the development of the steam carriage, for without some such provision it would have been impossible to produce enough steam generating power within the weight limitations required to make such vehicles practicable. As to the actual propelling machinery, Read had in mind two double-acting steam engines, each working one of the rear wheels through a rack and pinion drive, so that either could be used to turn the carriage under power. In 1791 he finally obtained a patent relating to his boiler, yet the idea remained in obscurity for many years and appears to have had little if any bearing on the development of early steam vehicles.

Back in England, the application of steam power to road carriages had, by 1801, outstripped the experimental stage. That year, William Trevithick built the first motorcar specifically designed to carry passengers. Perched high on giant wheels 10 feet in diameter and geared to a counter shaft which was driven by a steam cylinder with double piston rods, Trevithick's carriage mounted a wrought iron boiler located at the back. Though crude and elementary in various respects, it could carry eight passengers and frequently achieved a speed of 10 mph—being the first self-propelled vehicle ever to do so. Not bad for the time, yet despite several satisfactory trials Trevithick could find no backers and eventually ran out of funds. Compelled by necessity, he took the engine out of his carriage, and sold it to a hoop rolling mill where it drove the machinery for many years.

Two years later, a steam engine built to the inventor's specifications was attached to a coach which plied the streets in London as an omnibus with fair success. Trouble started when the carriage tore down a garden wall and the driver was pelted with rotten eggs, cabbages and tomatoes; but this probably had little to do with the fact that in 1804 Trevithick gave up his attempts at road locomotion and turned his attention to railroads.

Meantime, an American engineer named Oliver Evans from Delaware, Pa., really was setting agog the minds of men with his

The James and Anderson Steam Carriage of 1829 had two steam engines (one for each wheel) and could lug three tons at 15 mph, a good clip. Designer William James, however, ran out of funds.

mechanical and steam powered inventions. Starting with a vibrating engine and boiler in 1792, he designed a candle molding machine and a screw mill, both in 1795 and patented burr mill stones two years later. Then, in 1801, he began work on perhaps his most far-reaching and certainly his most spectacular brain child—the "Orukter Amphibolis" or Amphibious Digger. This juggernaut was in reality a huge steam-powered, flat-bottomed craft commissioned by the Philadelphia Board of Health for digging either by land or water and deepening the docks of the city. Since, however, it was equipped with wheels and could travel over land under its own steam, Evans rightly claimed the distinction of being the very first American to design, build and actually run a steam-powered "carriage."

Early in July 1805, this monster—30 feet long, 12 feet wide and weighing 34,437 pounds—was completed and ready for launching. Specifications are worth re-

cording in some detail. Provided with steam by a vast tubular type boiler, the vertical drop-valve engine had a cylinder 5x19 in. with a piston rod connected to an overhead wooden beam near one end. The other end of the beam was suspended by a movable link to permit it to move up and down, parallel with the piston. A gigantic flywheel kept the engine's rotation at a steady pace, power being applied to a paddle wheel suspended from the stern of the body. In addition, however, Evans installed enormous iron-tired wooden carriage wheels on the craft and drove them on one side by a system of belts.

On the day set for launching, disaster overtook Evans's machine when the road wheels broke down under the tremendous strain and new ones had to be made and fitted. The workmen engaged on the project undertook to do this without wages and Evans hit on another way of compensating them. In readiness for July 13, the day of the actual successful launching, Evans had

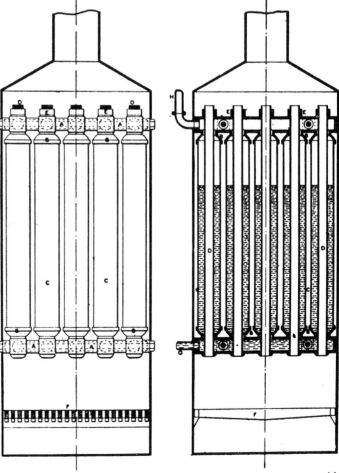

This high-pressure, multitubular boiler designed in 1830 by Summers and Ogle was a big improvement in steam generators. Their Phaeton would do 32 mph.

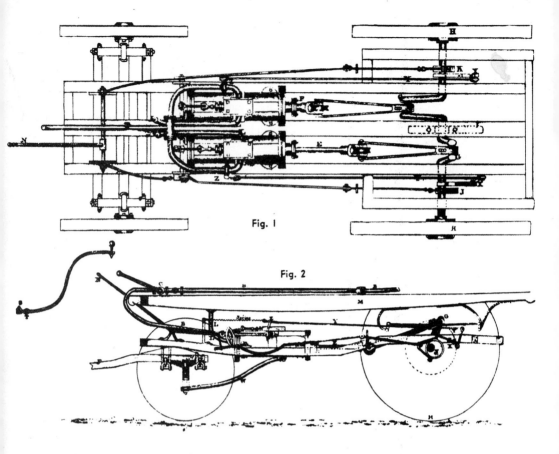

Fig. 1

Fig. 2

This original design of the Gurney Steamer, above, was drafted in 1827. It gave no hint of the complex superstructure or the top-heavy boiler. It was much modified during the next four years.

posters printed and circulated, inviting the public to inspect his Amphibious Digger. "The above machine," he told them, "is now to be seen moving around the Center Square (in Philadelphia) at the expense of the workmen who expect 25c from every generous person who may come to see the operation; but all are invited to come and view it, those who cannot as well as those who can conveniently spare the money."

How many of the awe-stricken onlookers could "conveniently spare" 25c is not recorded, but certain it was that a vast crowd converged on Center Square to get a close look at this monstrous curiosity, and that those who paid got their money's worth. Amid the hiss of steam, the groans and cracks of tortured wood, the rhythmic clanging of the engine and the shouts of the workmen mingled with the exhortations of the crowd, Oliver Evans and his "Orukter Amphibolis" jarred into motion, faltered, got under way and finally covered

1½ miles under steam power to the Schulkill River where the launching took place. The land speed was not disclosed, but once the craft became waterborne and the engine resumed its function of driving the paddle wheel, it made a steady four mph on its way up to the Philadelphia waterfront. Thus was the first motorcar successfully run in America.

But Oliver Evans was not through yet. There remained many other things for him to accomplish and his philosophy carries a pretty authentic note, even today. "When we see a man, one of the first ideas that strikes our minds is that he can know but little more than ourselves."

Evans, in fact, knew quite a "little more." Besides his drop valve engine, he had designed a high pressure steam engine and boiler between 1802 and 1804; and an illuminating gas generator the year before his amphibious steam carriage came to life. By 1811 he also was responsible for a rotary valve Columbian steam engine, whence he proceeded with other inventions.

In 1808, three years after the first American steam carriage, an Englishman —Dumbell by name—patented a steam vehicle with a peculiar boiler which evidently held the germ of the modern flash-type generator. The inventor proposed raising steam by allowing water to drop on an iron plate kept red hot by a fire which was forced by a pair of bellows. At first sight, perhaps a not very startling idea, but certainly a far-reaching one.

Next on the English scene of steam propulsion was one Julius Griffith of Brompton who in 1821 came out with a handsome but rather complicated steam carriage driven from astern by a unit-built engine and water tube boiler. This carriage was manufactured by Bramah, the well-known engineer and lock-maker, to Griffith's specifications and the design was patented not only in England but, in view of its "universal importance," also in Austria and America.

Griffith's Steam Carriage reached for some lofty objectives, being intended to carry three tons of merchandise at five mph with a saving of 25 per cent compared with horses. The two-cylinder engine featured an air-cooled condenser, while the boiler consisted of horizontal tubes extending across the firebox. Engine and boiler were ingeniously cushioned by spring suspension and the advent of this carriage was announced with a great flourish of trumpets. But then came the rub: in practice, the design of the boiler made it impossible to retain water in the lower tubes, and these repeatedly fell apart under the stress of the fire. Exit Julius Griffith, though not without having left his mark on the accident accented pages recording the development of the steam car.

The next practical attempt along these lines took place in Scotland in 1824, when two gentlemen from Leith, named Burstall and Hill, took out a patent for a flash-type boiler. This consisted of several trays heated to a temperature of 500° F. Water was injected past the trays whenever steam was needed and was kept under air pressure to enable it to flow into the boiler without the use of a feed pump. A muffler was used to deaden the sound of the exhausted steam, but it appears that the transmission of this carriage was needlessly complicated in an attempt to secure four-wheel drive. The front axle was driven from the rear axle by means of a shaft and two sets of bevel gears—an arrangement that was bound to offer certain steering and traction problems. These were partly overcome by providing the wheel bosses (hubs) with ratchet clutches to allow the outer wheel to travel faster on corners. Lugging a weight of about six tons, the Burstall and Hill carriage could make only some four mph and was not considered a success. Much as its predecessors, this machine, too, fell a victim to the shortcomings of its inventors in the fields of metallurgy and thermo-dynamics. It embodied several good ideas but they simply did not work out in practice.

But if the year 1824 was one of failure for the Scottish inventors, it certainly heralded the start of achievement for an Englishman named Walter Hancock. Without question, Hancock proved the most successful of the early steam carriage builders. Between 1824 and 1840, this versatile designer produced no less than nine steam carriages, of which the most successful—the "Autopsy" appeared in 1833. Not the least virtue of this machine was that in appearance it broke away from traditional attempts to build steam-powered vehicles that looked like horse-drawn carriages without horses. Hancock used plenty of imagination. For example, he located the passenger compartment forward and the boiler at the back, placing the engine between the two in an attempt to distribute weight correctly. The engine was a two-cylinder, vertical job with its crankshaft connected to the rear wheels by enclosed chain gearing. The chain wheel on the crankshaft was provided with a clutch to allow the engine to run free when the car was stationary, so that the fan and boiler feed pump could be kept working. The boiler, which Hancock regarded as his most important invention, consisted of flat rectangular chambers placed vertically above a fire grate. These chambers were two inches thick and so spaced as to allow passages for the flames from the fire grate. Working steam pressure was 100 pounds per square inch and draft was produced by an engine-driven fan. The road wheels were of wood with metal tires, and the "Autopsy" was an excellent performer. It could, for instance, tackle a 1 in 20 grade with ease, "even during a severe frost succeeding a shower of sleet which had completely glazed the road so that horses could hardly keep their feet."

To prove its reliability, Hancock once drove the "Autopsy" all the way from London to Brighton, a distance of 50 miles; but being designed as an omnibus it fulfilled this purpose admirably by plying the streets of London for a considerable time between the districts of Pentonville and Finsbury Square. Yet, ironically enough, while Hancock's steam carriages were successful mechanically, they proved something of a commercial failure. Too much prejudice against a new-fangled means of locomotion was still rampant.

During this epoch, most of the practical attempts at building steam cars seemed to be originating in England, and it is recorded that Nevill's Steam Carriage fashioned a year after Hancock got into his stride (in 1825), was the first to use an oscillating cylinder engine. Apparently nothing much came of this endeavor.

Next in the long line of British steam propulsion pioneers was one William H. James who in 1829 built a coach along lines indicated in a patent which he had obtained in 1823. This machine was quite an ambitious undertaking. It featured a twin-cylinder engine for *each* of the rear driving wheels and two high-pressure water-tube boilers that could supply an aggregate 200 pounds of working steam. The engines, swung on the main axle, were supported by springs at the ends of the cylinders, a system much later adopted with great success by the Stanley brothers. The throttle valves of the two engines were connected with the steering gear in such a way that steam was cut down on the inside engine when making a turn, but admitted equally to each engine while the carriage went straight ahead. With each boiler, 4½ feet long, supplying its own engine, James' steam coach could make 15 mph, despite a weight of three tons which included 15 passengers. During tests made with a full load, the machine actually sustained this speed on a rough gravel road in Epping Forest, purposely chosen.

The advantage of using two separate boilers also was demonstrated on an occasion when one of the boilers gave out and the carriage still reached home on a single engine, keeping a steady seven mph.

The reason why five long years elapsed between the time James first obtained his patents and the building of his carriage, was the usual one. The inventor had considerable trouble with his plans owing to what he amusingly termed "a deficiency of that metallic medium which is indispensable to the culture of steam carriages." It was not until late in 1828, when he secured Sir James Anderson as a financial backer, that James was able to get things under way. But there were functional problems, too. Despite its promising performance, the James and Anderson Steam Carriage suffered from chronic boiler trouble. The ordinary gas piping used for the tubes was not equal to the steam pressures imposed and continually gave way at the seams.

Undaunted, James battled steadily with this bug and even tried stepping up steam pressure to 300 pounds, but the workmanship of that time couldn't stand the strain. Next, he experimented with an oscillating steam engine, only to run out once more of that "metallic medium."

Though Sir James Anderson would extend no further backing, he became so interested in the idea of steam propulsion that he turned into an inventor himself, and nine years later (in 1838) produced

Sir Goldworthy Gurney's 1831 Steam Coach was one of several that carried over three thousand passengers four thousand miles without serious trouble. Leaking boilers were harmless problem.

a new boiler and formed the Steam Wagon and Carriage Company.

In 1830, two more Englishmen—William Alltoft Summers and Nathaniel Ogle—appeared on the scene with a vastly improved form of multi-tubular boiler which they installed in a steam carriage of their design a year later. Much attention was given to the boiler because the partners had in mind two specific objectives which they clearly laid down ahead of time. The first was to devise "a safe method of generating steam in sufficient quantity at all times to propel vehicles on common roads at any desired speed, and with such command of power as will overcome increased resistance from occasional obstacles, fresh graveled, soft or hilly roads." Secondly they envisaged "the safe application of this power to vehicles of such construction as will discover action and progress on any description of ground, and nevertheless be under immediate control and certain guidance of the conductor."

With these ideals in mind, Summers and Ogle built in 1831 a treble-bodied Phaeton which heralded the first year of the commercial application of steam to road locomotion. Specifications were as follows:

Engine: Two-cylinder, 20 hp, coupled direct to a cranked driving axle that rotated rear wheels 5 ft. 6 in. in diameter. Bore 7½ in.; stroke 18 in.

Boiler: Water tube type with 30 double tubes; 250 sq. ft. of heating surface; 247 pounds of working steam pressure. Rear location. Draft by engine-driven fan.

The chassis was a three-wheeled affair with a single front wheel doing the steering, and the boiler which was carried on a frame behind and separate from the carriage body, evaporated seven pounds of water for every pound of coke burned. Despite a weight of three tons with coal and water but no passengers, the Summers and Ogle Steam Coach was so efficient that it could average better than 24 mph with a full load and had a maximum speed of 32 to 35 mph. Unquestionably, this made it by far the fastest steam car of that epoch —a characteristic retained in later vehicles built by these two engineers.

A second carriage produced in 1832 had a three-cylinder engine and easily averaged 15 mph with a load of 19 passengers, traveling from Liverpool to Southampton with "great success."

If anything is evident from the foregoing, it is much less the fact that Summers and Ogle had latched on to any startling new discovery, than that they paid great attention to detail, thought things out beforehand and exercised meticulous care in the construction of their carriage. In a word, progress was asserting itself.

Simultaneously, yet another Englishman, Sir Goldsworthy Gurney, also was making headlines of the day in matters relating to steam-powered road transportation. Sir Goldsworthy was the most spectacular, if not the most successful steam carriage builder of that period, and his first machine—completed in 1831—even was equipped with steam driven feet in-

Walter Hancock's famous 1833 "Autopsy" carried a load of six passengers plus driver and stoker. In addition it hauled a trailer with a load of eight persons. Hancock used plenty of imagination.

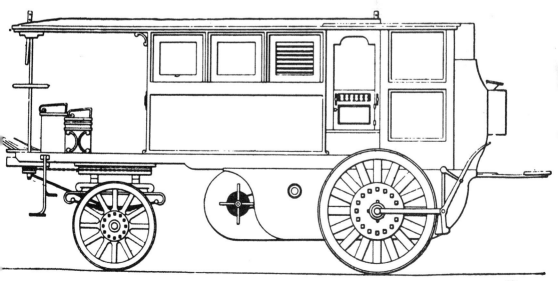

Church's Steam Coach, 1833, couldn't take the beating imposed by the terrible "roads" of the day.

tended to push the carriage uphill when the wheels slipped. Needless to say this idea was soon abandoned, but the Gurney Steam Coach embodied much else that was both interesting and meritorious. Driven by two single-cylinder horizontal engines with a bore and stroke of 9x18 in., it derived steam from a water tube boiler featuring a fusible plug to guard against burst tubes. Working steam pressure was 70 to 120 pounds, the engine was located amidships, under the body of the carriage. Direct drive to a cranked rear axle was used, but the wheels were driven by ratchets to permit the coach to turn corners more easily. A fifth wheel mounted in front served the sole purpose of acting as a pilot steering wheel. At first, a forced draft induced by a fan was employed to keep the fire going, but later it was found that enough draft could be obtained by passing the exhaust steam through the stack and the fan was dispensed with.

Fuel and water consumption of the Gurney steamer were fairly heavy—it evaporated 10 gallons of water and burned 20 pounds of coke for every mile covered—but considering its 7,580-pound weight with 14-passenger payload, performance was quite good. The original Gurney carriage covered its first six miles from Sir Goldsworthy's workshop near Regent's Park to the Edgware Road in 35 minutes; an average of better than 10 mph.

Gurney was no newcomer lucky enough to hit the jackpot first time off with a successful idea. He had been experimenting with, designing and testing steam vehicles since 1827, fully five years before his first commercial carriage became a reality. Now, encouraged by practical results, he went ahead and built several more steam coaches patterned on the first. For an unbroken period of at least four months, these carriages were a familiar sight between Gloucester and Cheltenham, performing a nine-mile trip four times daily and usually taking 55 minutes for the journey (9.8 mph), but often doing it in 45 minutes—12 mph. During this period, Sir Goldsworthy's machines were said to have carried some 3,000 passengers over a distance of more than 4,000 miles without any serious accidents. Delays were occasioned mostly by leaking boiler tubes—a harmless enough nuisance.

On one occasion, to demonstrate the reliability of his design, Sir Goldsworthy himself drove one of his steam coaches a distance of 84 miles in 10 hours, including all stops; yet the public still was not convinced and the colorful Gurney vehicles faded from sight.

The year 1831 must have been a busy one, however, among English advocates of steam propulsion on roadways, for besides Summers, Ogle and Gurney, an engineer named Surrey developed a steam tractor unit with the machinery separate from the main body of the carriage, so that the passengers were towed behind.

Barely two years passed before Dr. Church of Birmingham, England, turned up with a very ornate steam coach that had room enough for 40 passengers and a speed of about 15 mph. Alas, next to adverse legislation, the so-called "roads" of the time were the toughest thing cars had to contend with. The surface usually was so bad that it would have been hard on a modern traction engine traveling at, say, six mph; and when Church attempted to hold 15 and even 20 mph, the wear and tear on the machinery of his carriage was tremendous.

In building a stout three-wheeler with spring steel wheels 8 ft. 6 in. in diameter and 12 to 18 in. wide, it would seem that Church made some allowance for the appalling road conditions, but that allowance was not sufficient. The machine completed a few trial runs but was never commissioned into service. Design-wise, Church's Steam Coach featured no epoch-making novelty. The rear wheels were mounted on separate axles, chain driven from the engine crank, while the boiler (located astern) consisted of double tubes arranged vertically around a central fire box. The machine originally was built for the London and Birmingham Steam Carriage Co., whose continued existence appears to have been somewhat in doubt.

By 1834, Scotland again came to the fore when John Scott Russell built several steam cars for service between Glasgow and Paisley, a distance of about 7½ miles which took 40 to 45 minutes—an average of 10 mph. Russell was well-known in connection with the design of the steamship "Great Eastern," which later met with a sad ending; but the impending doom of that gigantic flop could hardly be said to reflect unfavorably on Russell's abilities as an engineer. The ship was simply too big while contemporary knowledge of metallurgy and mechanics was, conversely, too small.

But to return to his steam coaches: these were built to Russell's design by an Edinborough firm and were of conventional enough construction. Steam was supplied

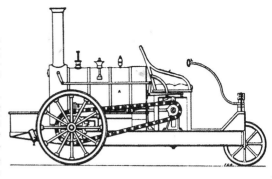

Rickett's Road Steamer looked like a locomotive going backward in 1858. It could do over 12 mph.

by a multi-tubular boiler to a two-cylinder vertical engine, the crankshaft of which drove the rear axle by spur wheels.

These coaches were very popular, nevertheless, often carrying as many as 35 passengers to a load, which was close crowding, considering these machines were intended for 20 people outside and six inside.

The next notable road steamer to appear in England did so after a lapse of nearly a quarter of a century, in 1858. This machine, designed and built by the Thomas Rickett Castle Foundry in Buckingham, to the order of the Marquess of Stafford, was really a steam road locomotive and made no pretense at looking like anything else. Supported on three wheels with the single front wheel doing the steering, it was driven by a horizontal two-cylinder engine of 3x9 in. bore and stroke which gave it a road speed of 10 mph at 220 rpm with a gear ratio of 2.5 to 1. Rear-mounted, the engine had piston rods which drove small sprocket wheels or pinions, and these in turn drove larger sprockets on the rear wheels by means of chains. Normally, only one rear wheel took up the drive, but on stiff hills or bad roads the other wheel could be turned into a driver as well by means of a clutch. On curves, however, it was necessary to disengage this clutch for obvious reasons.

The boiler of Rickett's Road Steamer was of the return tube type with an integral firebox and an uptake at the rear. It delivered steam at a working pressure of 100 pounds—enough to attain a speed of about 12 mph. The main wheels were of iron with wood rims and iron tires, a friction type brake acting on both main wheels. Weight was 3,470 pounds, fueled and ready to go, but without driver or passenger.

Two years later, in 1860, Rickett built an improved road steamer for the Earl of Gaithness; following this he came up with

Dudgeon's heavy looking Steam Wagon, first on New York streets in 1860, scared horses and people alike with its terrible sound and fury.

A steam auto builder for over thirty-five years, Stephen Roper perfected this steam bicycle in 1894. It would go 60 mph, was a compact marvel.

First of three experimental horseless carriages built by Ransom E. Olds, this 1887 steam buggy was the brainchild of one of industry's greats.

a machine which he sold to Spain where it was used as a light omnibus traction engine.

That year was also of particular interest to Americans, for it marked the advent of the first steam wagon to appear in the streets of New York. Its inventor was Richard Dudgeon, who copied without apologies the basic layout of the steam locomotive as being the most practical design.

Dudgeon, who coupled an inventive and adventurous turn of mind with the ownership of a manufacturing establishment, was blessed with most of the facilities necessary to carry out his ideas. Calling his machine simply a Steam Wagon, he built it on a wooden four-wheel framework suitable for carrying a steam boiler. Water tanks on either side, extending along the length of the wagon, were covered with seat cushions offering seat space for eight or ten passengers.

The engine, consisting of two single cylinders located on the outside and each driving one rear wheel, was mounted obliquely and drove the rear axle directly via the piston rods. The bore was four inches and the stroke 16 in.—quite enough to pack a powerful wallop when fed from a high-pressure boiler tested to withstand steam at 250 pounds per square inch. The water capacity was small, limiting the range of the machine, and intense heat was required to generate steam—a condition not calculated to add to the comfort of the passengers, who already were riding on solid wooden wheels of red cedar bound with metal tires.

By degrees, however, Dudgeon solved these various problems and his Steam Wagon was the first of its kind ever to put in an appearance on Upper Broadway, New York City. There it proved such a terror to horses and human beings alike that the police compelled the inventor to take his machine home—as quickly as possible, please!

With steam exhausting at high pressure with a terrific noise, and the vehicle proceeding at a "lively gait," clanking, clattering and belching forth fire and smoke from a short stack, it is not difficult to imagine the fearsome effect this apparition must have had on denizens and animals alike.

Richard Dudgeon decided there was less public sentiment to overcome in the quiet village of Locust Valley, Long Island, where his country home was located, and accordingly moved his base of operations to that retreat. True, the country horses took no more kindly to the hissing, snort-

More ambitious was second Olds Steamer of 1891. The inventor, looking pleased, has left hand on steering tiller while right controls throttle. Note friction brake blocks for front wheels.

ing machine than did those of the city, but there were fewer of them around to be annoyed.

Apparently, steering the Dudgeon Steam Wagon was a matter of management that required considerable skill, even in the seclusion of rural areas with no traffic to worry about. A quarter turn of the steering rod was enough to make a "considerable variation from a straight course." Knowing just how much to turn the handle in order to round a curve or pass another vehicle without upsetting the machine required a skill which no living person but Mr. Dudgeon ever seemed able to master. And even he one day ran into a barber's shop at Oyster Bay.

The machine later appeared in Bridgeport, Conn., where Dudgeon received a special police permit to run it in the city streets; and here it soon became as well known as Barnum's Circus.

The original Dudgeon Steam Wagon was destroyed by fire when the Crystal Palace burned down in New York City; but the inventor built an exact duplicate which was used after his death by his son, Frank P. Dudgeon, who preserved the machine intact, save for a slightly larger boiler.

The next American manifestation in the steam vehicle world occurred in the year of grace 1870, when a Mr. Stephen H. Roper of Roxbury, Mass., built a steam powered bicycle which was both compact and practical and performed satisfactorily. Roper achieved the distinction of being the first American to construct such a machine, but

he already was an old hand at the game who had built several three- and four-wheeled steam cars since 1860.

While riding one of his steam cars through the streets of Boston in 1870, Roper was stopped by an angry Alderman who chanted, "You have no right to bring such a machine as that into the street to frighten the horses!" Roper calmly replied, "There is no law against it, sir," whereupon the Alderman vowed that if such was the case he would see there was one within 24 hours. Next day this busybody railroaded an ordinance through the Town Board, prohibiting steam vehicles from the city of Boston; but paradoxically this same Board had appropriated $5,000 a short time before to be applied on experiments "looking toward the perfecting of a self-propelled steam power engine." A member of the Board with a sense of humor pointed out to his colleagues the absurdity of their inconsistency, whereupon the foolish ordinance was promptly repealed.

Unperturbed, Stephen Roper built no less than 10 steam vehicles between 1860 and 1894, when he sold a four-wheeler weighing 325 pounds to a Mr. William Holmes who was a brick manufacturer in Boston. That year, too, he came out with a perfected version of his Steam Bicycle, mounted in a standard Columbia cycle frame. It was quite a machine and a marvel of neatness. Roper used a marine-type two-cylinder engine, 2x4 in., with the connecting rods "attached directly to the hind axle." At only 200 rpm, this power unit gave the bicycle a road speed of 60 mph, which it could have sustained indefinitely with almost no wear.

Even more remarkable was the boiler—a water tube type squeezed into a space 16x6x6 in., yet containing 70 tubes which produced steam at a pressure of 150 pounds. The water supply was carried in a long circular tank fastened to the top of the frame, under the saddle, and either kerosene or "gasolene" fuel could be used. Complete, less the rider, Roper's Steam Bicycle scaled only 70 pounds and in its day could outrun just about anything on the highway. The inventor could not properly be called a manufacturer, even though he made two or three scales, for none of his vehicles was built with a specific commercial intent. Each was by way of an experiment, now and again successful enough to attract a purchaser, but intended primarily for his own use.

Five years passed before, in 1871, a Doctor J. N. Carhart of Racine, Wisconsin, built a two-cylinder steam buggy which not only ran but, by appearing in the main street on market day, nearly threw the town into a panic. Its authenticity, however, was attested to by no less a person than the Secretary of State for Wisconsin, and Carhart's experiments aroused so much interest that the State Legislature passed an act in 1875, appropriating $10,000 as a bounty for the first inventor to produce a machine "propelled by steam or other motive agent," such machine to be "cheap and practical as a substitute for horses, on highway or farm." The bill also laid down certain specific requirements as to performance, climbing power and maneuver-ability. The upshot of the whole thing was an endurance run (in reality the first American road race) which attracted seven entries but brought only two starters. Run on a 201-mile course from Green Bay to Madison, Wisconsin, it was won by a steam buggy named the "Oshkosh" at an average of six mph. Though Doc Carhart's steamer was a non-starter, to him went the credit for running the first self-propelled light-weight vehicle on a US highway.

By 1887 a new star had arisen on the horizon of American steam propulsion. The visionary Ransom E. Olds had built a three-wheeled steam buggy of his own design and drove it early one morning through the streets of Lansing, Mich. He tactfully chose an early hour when the streets would be empty to avoid scaring horses and humans; the equine population was hardly likely to take into account the fact that the young inventor's father—Pliny F. Olds—was a prominent citizen who owned a stationary gas engine factory.

The first Olds steamer was a pretty rudimentary affair with a single-cylinder engine mounted in back and no attempt at anything much save to cover ground under its own power, which it did. Further, it had the virtue of a neat compactness conspicuously lacking in earlier vehicles of this type.

Pleased with the results, Ransom E. Olds went on to build a second steamer which he completed in 1891. Though not so tidy-looking as its predecessor, this machine was a more ambitious effort of four-wheeled construction with the engine and a large vertical water tube boiler mounted at the back. Steel-tired carriage wheels

"Dark Horse" was Vanell's Steam Carriage, entered in Chicago Times Herald Race of 1895. This turbine job, however, never got started.

were used, the front pair being set close together and steered by tiller. Some protection from the inclemencies of the weather was provided by a fringed canopy through which the boiler's smokestack exhausted. Weight was around 900 pounds and speed about five mph, though by no means in silence. Still, it traveled further, faster and more reliably than the prototype and the young inventor began to realize his consuming ambition to build motor vehicles. A year or so later, Olds built a third steamer with a flash-type boiler of his own design which apparently achieved worldwide fame through an article published in the Scientific American. As a result, this machine was purchased by the Francis Times Company of Bombay, India, and so became the first American-built horseless carriage to be exported. In addition, it probably was the first steam-powered American passenger automobile of any kind actually sold for cash to a customer.

The famous Chicago Times Herald Road Race, first of its kind, held November 2, 1895, from Chicago to Evanston, Ill., and back, attracted some 82 entries, all of them interesting in one way or another. Among them, lured by the first prize of $2,000 and a gold medal, was a steam carriage designed by an engineer named Frank Vanell of Vincennes, Indiana. Vanell had some highly original ideas, including an engine "on the rotary order" attached to the driving shaft "without gearing of any kind." Seems as though the inventor came up with some form of steam turbine—an idea by no means unlikely, even at this time. Steam was supplied by a vertical water-tube boiler mounted in front, and the wheels

Marine engineer John Einig toured Jacksonville, Fla., in this home-built lightweight (400 pound) Steam Buggy. The year was 1896.

Fine workmanship and sound design stamped this Cross Steamer of 1897. Rear engine drove front wheels through belts and gears. Mechanism was neatly enclosed. See photo top of following page.

were carried on steel axles with anti-friction bearings. The driving wheels measured five ft. in diameter and the steering wheels two ft., both sets having pneumatic tires. Steering was by sprocket wheel and chain through a tiller and Vanell estimated the all-up weight at 1,200 pounds. Cost of construction seemed moderate enough at $275, but there is no evidence that the machine ever ran—let alone made a start in the Times Herald race, even though it appeared in the final entry list.

The year following Vanell's somewhat elusive steam car (in 1896), John Einig, a marine engineer of Jacksonville, Florida, built a compact steam carriage with a vertical boiler slung under the body and a horizontal engine driving the rear wheels. Using "gasoline" for fuel, this machine could actually do 18 to 20 mph for a weight of about 400 pounds, excluding that of the two passengers. The rear (driving) wheels were 50 in. in diameter and the front wheels 48 in. Tread was 40 in. and solid rubber tires were used. Fuel consumption was 1½ quarts per hour. The inventor claimed that "the sound of escaping steam

is successfully muffled and the vapor itself is rendered invisible so that horses pay no attention to the carriage."

Despite these promising attributes, Einig offered his machine for sale at half price three months later, advertising it in The Horseless Age early in 1897. It may be that his wife objected to the idea.

That same year, A. T. Cross of Providence, Rhode Island, inventor of the Cross stenographic pen, built for his own use "an experimental steam carriage so constructed that other motive power can be substituted if desired." This machine was a first rate engineering job which bore evidence of considerable thought and held the seeds of several interesting ideas. For instance, "in order to lessen vibration" the motive power and axle were suspended from the frame by spiral (coil) springs, while body and passengers were in addition "supported by elliptical springs."

Too, the transmission system deserves mention. A brass internal gear "firmly clamped to each rear wheel" was driven by a silent fiber gear at the ends of a countershaft. This, in turn, was driven

A fine view of the enclosed Cross Steamer with weather-proof hood up; 1800 lbs., car went 10 mph.

from the engine by twin belts and pulleys.

Cross used a rear-mounted power unit consisting of two separate vertical cylinders, 2¼x2¼ in., with slide valve reverse motion but no links or eccentrics. The cylinders were of the oscillating type, produced about one hp each and would run at 400 rpm. A water-tube type boiler of wrought iron and steel, tested to 300 pounds, gave 150 pounds of steady working steam pressure. This was located in the middle of the carriage, behind the engine bulkhead. A "powerful foot brake acting on band pulleys" took care of the stopping, but it was found in practice that by merely reversing the engine the wheels could be made to "skid along a plank walk."

Two tanks, each of 15 gallons, held an adequate supply of water and kerosene; in fact there was enough water to run the machine for five hours, while the running cost with "crude petroleum" averaged out at about one cent per mile.

The Cross Steam Carriage weighed some 1,800 pounds and would make 10 mph without trouble for considerable periods. All in all it reflected the ideals of a meticulous engineer whose claim that he had been "interested in the motor vehicle problem for many years" was obviously true. It seems a pity that this steam car never actually went into production, for it would have found many buyers. In several respects it was superior to some of the contemporary steamers that were just beginning to be offered for sale to the public at about this time.

And so, with the closing of the nineteenth century, the story of pioneering and experimentation by isolated individuals fascinated with the possibilities of steam power in road vehicles comes to an end, both in the Old World and the New. An enormous amount of progress still remained to be made, and the battle between steam and internal combustion engines had barely begun—let alone been lost by the steamers. But in 1899, there were already in the United States some eight manufacturers of steam passenger vehicles engaged in the gainful business of building and selling these vehicles to an eager public. The commercial era of the steam car was rapidly gathering a full head of steam. •

25

1896-1925

The Stanley

Bearded Stanley Twins, F. E. and F.O., taken here in their first Steam Carriage in 1897, were destined to go places in the steam world. Carriage shown cost $700.

F.O. and F.E., the Stanley Twins, write their name in steam, watch it drift away.

THE STORY OF the Stanley Steamer is unique in the history of the automobile industry and colorful enough for a movie scenario. It has all the exciting ingredients of challenge, pioneering courage, imagination, patience, determination in the conquest of obstacles, and the gallant championship of a cause generally regarded as lost. To do it justice would require an entire book—but since we are attempting to cover a broader field, an outline will have to serve.

The story begins with the birth of the Stanley Twins, Francis E. and Freeland O.—later known simply as "F.E." and "F.O."—in Kingsland, Maine, on June 1, 1849. As they grew up almost indistinguishable from each other, even to their neatly trimmed beards and manner of dressing, it became apparent that they both had inherited the gift of inventiveness, though its expression took different forms. While "F.E." inclined toward the practical and developed into a "sort of all-around mechanical genius," twin "F.O." discovered academic tendencies and eventually became a

26

schoolteacher. Among their early activities, the Stanleys numbered some pretty unusual achievements, including the production of the first commercially manufactured violins in the US; the invention of a home generator for illuminating gas which sold well before the competitive advent of municipal gas works; the first practical manufacture of photographic dry plates at a time when photography was still in its infant stage; and the development of some early X-ray equipment.

Of all these, "F.E." visualized the greatest profit in photography and with less and $500 started a small dry-plate manufacturing business on his own at Lewistown, Maine, in 1875 at the age of 26. He did so well that in 10 years he managed to save $50,000 and with this—joined by brother "F.O." who dropped schoolteaching in 1885—started a much larger photographic firm in Newton, Mass., known as the Stanley Bros. Dry Plate Manufacturing Co.

Another prosperous decade went by for the Twins who, driven ever by a restless imagination, began to look around for something else into which to channel their inventive ability. They found it in the first stirrings of a movement toward the commercial production of "horseless carriages" propelled by steam. The idea finally crystallized in the fall of 1896 when the Twins attended Brockton Falls Fair, Mass., where a steam "horseless carriage" was due to perform. The exhibition was disappointing, the steamer breaking down before it even completed one lap of the course; but here was a challenge and something prompted "F.E." to say: "Well, boys, before another fall passes I will show you a self-propelled carriage that will go around that track not only once but several times without stopping!"

Having made this boast in public, there was nothing to do but go ahead and back it up; and that was exactly what the Stanleys did. But with typical thoroughness they took their time, "F.E." studying every available design before he came up with a set of specifications that held practical promise. The first Stanley Steamer was not begun until July 6, 1897, and completed in October of that year. The brothers made no attempt to build their own engine, but secured one best suited to their needs from J. W. Penny & Sons, Mechanic Falls, Mass. Other parts they obtained as required from various outside sources, so that the carriage was more of an assembled than a manufactured job; but the result was amazing.

The steamer performed just as predicted by "F.E.," making several easy rounds of the Brockton Fair course. The outcome was that the brothers immediately began work on three more steamers of similar design. One of these was sold to John Brisbane Walker of Cosmopolitan Magazine in 1898, who evinced tremendous enthusiasm and in turn sold it to a financier named Amzi L. Barber with the same effect. Seeing a big future in these steamers, Barber and Walker decided to buy out the Stanley brothers.

Meanwhile, "F.E." and "F.O." scored

This was the improved 1898 Stanley Steamer with which F.E. covered a mile in 2 min. 11 secs. around the Charles River Park Track, Cambridge, Mass. Weighing just over 400 pounds, car carried 12 gallons of water, eight of gasoline, enough for 23 miles. A working pressure of 150 psi could be built in 4½ minutes.

This redesigned 1900 Stanley Motor Carriage, below, built by the Stanley Mfg. Co., Lawrence, Mass., was "not to be confused with products of the Locomobile and Mobile companies and the Stanley brothers." Lines followed those of the Whitney Automatic Steamer, but the brothers were sued, nonetheless, by Locomobile.

their first big triumph on November 8, 1898 when they entered one of their early steamers in the Open-Air Horseless Carriage Meet held at Charles River Park, Cambridge, Mass., on a track ⅓ of a mile long. Before some 5,000 spectators jammed into the grandstand, the Stanleys drove their machine three times around the course in 2 min. 11 secs., covering the mile at an average of 27.40 mph. Then "F.E." went on to do two miles without trouble in 5 minutes and 19 seconds at 22.22 mph. Almost immediately 100 prospective customers rushed to place orders for this remarkable steamer.

In 1899 the brothers purchased an old bicycle factory where production of the Stanley started in earnest on a commercial scale. The schedule called for 100 steam cars with standardized interchangeable parts. The bodies arrived from "a maker of fine carriages" complete with leather dashboard and even a whip socket. From the fall of 1898 to the fall of 1899 Stanleys built and sold not 100 but 200 steamers and were the first in the world to manufacture automobiles in commercial quantities. "F.E." took this success with characteristic confidence and was even casual about it. Said he: "It is not necessary to make use of any patent or invention

Happier days were when Mr. and Mrs. F.O. had just completed the grueling climb up Mount Washington on August 31, 1899, left. Theirs was the first horseless carriage ever to complete the big climb.

Produced late in 1902 this Stanley Steam Carriage was really an early 1903 model. Making its debut in competition in September, 1902, it stole the limelight during the Rhode Island Automobile Club meet held at Naragansett Track; came in third.

in order to turn out a practical motor carriage. The common sense use of known principles is all that is required." To an interested press photographer who pointed out the risk, "F.E." said: "Go on and take your pictures. We'll patent nothing."

He changed his mind, however, when persistently approached by Walker and Barber to sell out, and duly secured his carriage with the necessary protective patents. To Barber, the phenomenal success of the Stanley was the clincher. It made the enterprise even more desirable than before, and by the summer of 1899 he and Walker had purchased all the Stanley patents, good will and manufacturing facilities (including 100 wagons "on the way") for $250,000 and formed the Locomobile Co. of America with the object of manufacturing the Stanley under the new name.

Under the terms of the sale, the Stanley brothers undertook not to build any steam cars of their own for two years, the contract expiring May 1, 1900; but Walker and Barber had other troubles. Their rift in 1899 and the split of the new firm into two separate entities described elsewhere (see Locomobile story), actually proved beneficial to the twins, for each became a consulting engineer with one of the rival companies—"F.E." going with Locomobile and "F.O." to Mobile.

The year 1899 was a highly profitable one for the Stanleys. In addition to the Locomobile sale they disposed of their photographic business for a large sum to the Eastman Kodak Co. Money, certainly, was not one of their problems. That year, too, Mr. and Mrs. F. O. Stanley tackled the first climb of Mt. Washington by a self-propelled vehicle on August 31. It took them 2 hrs. 10 min. to reach the top, but to the greater glory of the steamer they made it safely.

But the Twins grew restless. They had enjoyed making their steamers and they had only sold out under approaches so persistent and determined that the buyers would brook no refusal. They had set the figure at a quarter of a million dollars, confident that Barber and Walker would back down but their price had been paid without argument. And now they wanted to build more steam cars. To circumvent the problem of the patent sale, "F.E." spent a year redesigning the whole machine, and when at the close of 1900 the Stanley Mfg. Co. of Lawrence, Mass., came into being, was careful to make this formal announcement: "The Stanley Mfg. Co. should not be confused with the Locomobile Co., the

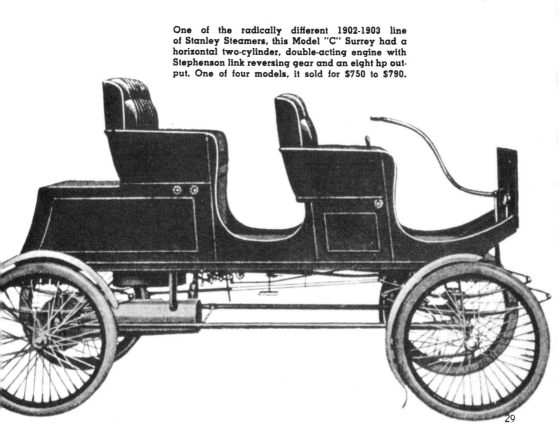

One of the radically different 1902-1903 line of Stanley Steamers, this Model "C" Surrey had a horizontal two-cylinder, double-acting engine with Stephenson link reversing gear and an eight hp output. One of four models, it sold for $750 to $790.

The Boston, Mass., police department made good use of the first police cars in the country. Driver's job was considerably less strenuous than cyclist's.

Encased in a sheet metal dust proof case, this 1903 two-cylinder horizontal Stanley engine was light, compact and geared directly to rear axle.

Mobile Co., nor the Stanley Brothers, all connected with the name Stanley and all employing steam as a mode of power, utilizing what has popularly become known as the "Stanley Type" boiler and engine. Frank F. Stanley is the chief owner of the Stanley Mfg. Co., where the McKay Sewing Machines for shoes are made. This company, as is well known to the trade, is licensed to operate under the patents of George E. Whitney. To avoid confusion with other builders, the company has decided to market its product under the trade name of McKay, a name already well known to those acquainted with the Stanley Mfg. Co. that has built the McKay shoe machinery for many years. . ."

Apparently, everything seemed all right. The Stanleys had obtained a whole new set of patents and, technically at least, there was no breach of the agreement relating to the Locomobile sale. But when the first of the new "Stanley" Motor Carriages appeared, the lid blew off. Outraged by what it considered an act of moral duplicity and bad faith, the Locomobile Company yelled the equivalent of "We wuz robbed!" What was more, there seemed to be a point of fact involved. A small part on the chain-tensioning device of the new "Stanley" was the same as that covered by the original patents purchased by the Locomobile Co.

Threatened with a whale-sized law suit, the Stanleys took the wisest course. Rather than embark on costly litigation, they completely redesigned the transmission of their new car, using direct drive and a horizontal engine to go with it. This naturally took time, and though the Stanley Motor Carriage Co. was formed in the spring of 1901, production did not get under way until the fall of that year. By October, the original agreement with Locomobile having lapsed, the Twins bought back all their original patents for a fraction of the sum they had received and were now free to use chain drive if they wished. They availed themselves of the opportunity while perfecting the direct drive transmission, which was not ready for production until May 1902. The way things turned out, the Stanleys built and sold 100 steam wagons at $600 each between October 1901 and September 1902, without showing a penny profit. Constant experiments, changes and improvements absorbed every penny they made.

But in 1902 the outlook for steamers generally was still very promising. Of the 909 automobiles registered in New York State alone, 485 were steam cars, mainly of Stanley, Locomobile, Mobile and White origin.

Things really got under way in 1903, by

Another Massachusetts first. This 1903 Model BX Stanley with folding front seat came complete with fire extinguishers and tools. Shown are Chief Randlett and Fireman Fogwell of Newton, Mass.

The 1904 Stanleys were strengthened against distortion by underframe triangular bracing. Equipped with a ten gallon fuel tank—enough for 160 miles on gasoline or 200 miles on paraffin, this Model EX weighed 1,008 pounds, had folding front seat.

31

A stripped Model "G" Stanley Gentleman's Speedy Roadster easily climbed Mount Washington non-stop with two passengers in 1905. In the background, over the Great Gulf, are Mts. Jefferson and Adams.

which time the Stanley Motor Carriage Co., had become the Stanley Bros. Mfg. Co., Newton, Mass., with 140 hands on the payroll, turning out and selling three wagons a day without the help of any advertising. "F.E." rightly believed that the recommendation of the satisfied user is the most effective form of advertising, and this view was one that he preserved even after multi-million dollar ad agencies had become a necessary and accepted part of business. In 1903, for instance, a Dr. C. A.

Dennett of Arlington, Mass., drove a Stanley 1,000 miles on a vacation through Maine without making a single trouble stop. Naturally, he told everyone about it; and what could be a better advertisement than his enthusiasm? To comments by automotive writers of the day, which sometimes contained double-edged praise that was a form of backhanded criticism, the Stanleys paid no attention at all.

For instance: "The 13 hand-operated valves of the Stanley Steamer and the com-

plexity of the firing up would appear to take a week of training by a competent steam engineer. The fact is that this complexity of hand valves and regulating devices works so perfectly, are so conveniently located and operate in such harmonious and logical sequence that any person of ordinary intelligence learns the lesson of their use easily and quickly." To which "F.E." mentally replied: "So what?"

The four Stanley models offered that year—B, C, BX and CX, the latter two with 16-in. boilers and a working steam pressure of 350 to 600 pounds—were selling like the proverbial hot cakes. On May 30, 1903, the first Stanley "Wogglebug" racing car appeared at Readville Track near Boston, painted red and shaped like a cigar for low wind resistance. It made the Mile in 1 minute, 2⅘ seconds at 21.09 mph—beating another steam car (the Cannon) by 2 seconds but as usual was damned by gas auto owners who dubbed it a "freak."

The first gas-powered automobile to conquer Mount Washington had done so in September 1902, over three years after F.O. Stanley's successful pioneer climb with a steamer. In 1904, "F.E." took a Model EX up in 27 minutes, filling the "opposition" with dismay.

Stanleys were now selling steadily at the rate of about 1,000 a year, even though steamers had lost the commercial battle with their gasoline rivals. The Twins, encouraged by competitive successes, produced a Florida racer late in 1905 from which were evolved the 1906 Vanderbilt Cup Stanleys, designed for but never run in that event. This was a powerful job with a 4½x6½-in. two-cylinder engine and a 30-in. boiler. It was geared-up 2 to 1 so that at 60 mph the engine turned very slowly—well below maximum efficiency.

Power was stepped up to 10 hp on this 1905 Model "E" Stanley Runabout by increasing cylinder size to 3x4 in. Model featured folding rear seat. Price was $850.00.

Vanderbilt Cup steamer was developed from same engine as the Florida Racers. Car never entered race for which it was named.

This factory-built 1906 Stanley "Beetle" racing steamer set five world records at Ormond Beach. Fred Marriott was driver.

At right is shown the "Beetle" speeding toward the finish line on Florida sands. Crossed line at timed average of 127.66 mph.

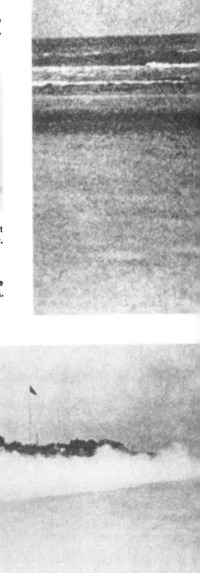

In 1905 Louis S. Ross drove his Stanley "Teakettle" over the measured Mile at 94.73 mph within 38 seconds. Steam generated at 600 psi explained performance. Power unit inspired the Florida Racers.

The following year, driven by F.E. Stanley with his son R.W. as passenger, this machine easily beat Walter Christie's famous front-drive gas car at Daytona Beach, Fla. in a match race. Meantime, in January 1906, the Florida steam racer driven by Fred Marriott had achieved a fantastic timed speed of 127.66 mph at Ormond Beach, Fla., being the first machine ever to propel a human being at over two miles a minute.

In the stock car class Stanley Steamers met with equal success, the 1906 Model H Gentlemen's Speedy Roadster claiming the title of Fastest Stock Car in the World, after winning a 15 mile handicap race at Ormond Beach in 13 min. 12 secs. (68.18 mph) and beating its nearest competitors by 4 to 5 *minutes,* "without going to the expense of importing a $10,000 racing machine."

Fred Marriott's miraculous escape from the record-breaking Stanley "Beetle" crash at Ormond in 1907 rather cooled the Twins' ardor for racing; but production for the year was maintained at a satisfactory 600 to 700 cars. The first closed Stanley Steamer made its appearance in the guise of the Model J Limousine with coachwork by the Currier Cameron Co., Amesbury, Mass. These were carriage builders —which explained why it looked like "a horse-drawn hack." Actually, this body style was built primarily for the use of Mrs. F.E., but found quite a few outside customers.

Eight models were on offer that year with a choice of two engines—the 30 hp job of similar bore and stroke to the Florida and Vanderbilt racer, and a 20 hp machine. A 26 in. boiler was used on the larger cars and a 23 in. one on the smaller models.

Principal change for 1908 was the introduction of a Model M with a 114 in. wheelbase and a roomy Touring body, that yet could be driven at *60* mph as long as the road permitted.

35

A twisted scrapheap was all that remained of "Beetle" in 1907 when Marriott hit a small depression, flew 100 feet through the air at almost 190 mph. Although Marriott was badly injured, he still is around.

The sporty 1906 Model "H" Fast Touring Car was equipped with previous year's 20 hp Model "F" engine. Weight was 1,350 pounds for a wheelbase of 100 in. Wire wheels carried 34x3 in. tires. Running gear was same as "F." Price, $1,000.

In 1908 the Stanley firm announced some new "more powerful" models. One of them was husky Model "M" Touring Car of 114 in. wheelbase which seated five. 60 mph speed was advertised. Price was $1,500.

Popular in 1909 was the Model 88 Mountain Wagon, seating 12 passengers, which owed its origin to the exclusive Stanley Hotel built by the brothers at Estes Park in the heart of the Colorado Rockies. It had earlier been developed mainly for use between Loveland Station and Estes Park, toting visitors 34 miles uphill to that magnificent scenic spot; but later was sold to many other users. The engine was a "detuned" and lower-geared version of the famous Florida racer power unit, capable of tremendous hauling power.

Few changes marked the period 1909 to 1912, except the introduction of a Torpedo-type, hand-made aluminum body used on the Model 73 of 1911, "made in the same factory that makes bodies for some of the best $5,000 and $6,000 cars in America." But even at this comparatively late date, the Stanley brothers still clung to a wooden chassis frame when practically all other auto manufacturers had gone to pressed steel.

By 1914, when World War I broke out, Stanleys had a redesigned engine with cranks at 45° to one another, obviating dead center and the need of a flywheel. For the sake of simplicity, the number of moving parts was reduced to 13, yet with gains in efficiency, lightness and power. A year later the firm adopted a new V-type radiator-condenser and lengthened the wheelbase by 10 in. to 130 in. for still greater riding comfort. The wooden chassis was finally discarded in favor of a channel steel frame and an improved driller burner replaced the former slot type. The brakes, too, were larger and more powerful to cope with added weight.

Extolling the virtues of the Stanley Steam Roadster Model 726 for 1916, a rare company ad commented: "The engine gets as many impulses per revolution as the conventional eight-cylinder gasoline engine. For several years Stanley owners have enjoyed the privilege of using kerosene for fuel, and the entire control of the Stanley is between two fingers of one hand. The present confusing market which confronts the purchaser of a motor car is so absurd and contradictory that it must be an exasperating experiment to try to determine which car to buy. The Stanley uses no clutches, gear-shifts, flywheels, carburetors, magnetos, spark plugs, distributors, self-starters or any of the marvelously ingenious complications with which inventors have had to overcome the difficulties inherent in the explosive engine. That is why 90 per cent of Stanley owners drive their cars without the assistance of trained chauffeurs."

In 1917 the firm discontinued the manufacture of commercial vehicles and offered only a 130 in. wheelbase chassis with three, five and seven passenger bodies "to give the factory an opportunity to keep pace with the demand for passenger cars." In May of that year, a notable and sad event occurred in the long life of the Stanley Motor Carriage Co. The famous brothers, "F.E." and "F.O.," retired and the business was reorganized and taken over by a new group, with Prescott Warren as president. Mr. F.E. survived his retirement by only

Model FX 1907 Runabout went 40 to 45 mph. Fuel tank was located in rear and weight was 1,100 pounds. Carried 40 to 50 mile water supply. Steamer sold for $850.00.

37

14 months. Returning alone from a trip to Maine, he was involved in a serious auto accident near Ipswich, Mass., and died on July 21, 1918, at the age of 70.

The Stanley Steamer of 1918 stood not quite alone in its field, but very nearly so. The White had long since joined the ranks of the gasoline rivals, and the Stanley's only companion was the comparatively recent Doble Steam Car which seemed, for the moment, to be doing pretty well.

That the Stanley company recognized its position as the last remaining steam-powered old-timer was evidenced by comments such as this: "Stanleys have been built for 20 years and the two biggest civilizing influences of all time—the steamship and the locomotive—are and always have been steam-propelled. Steam power is used, not because nothing else has been tried, but because everything else has been tried. Stanley cars have a longer life than cars of any other type, and country roads, city boulevards or busy streets are all alike to it. It is endowed with all the comfort and gentleness desired for a womanly woman. . ."

More than anything else, perhaps, this postscript told its own story: "Every Stanley owner is proud, secretly, that he had the courage of his convictions to buy an unconventional article, and the performance of the car has justified his judgment."

Chief detail innovation for 1918 was the use of an "electrically heated and ignited pilot burner," which derived current from a Willard Storage Battery. A step ahead.

During the remaining years of its active production life, the Stanley Steamer continued to use a time-tried, horizontal, two-cylinder, double-acting engine and to point out repeatedly, with unassailable logic, the superiority of the steam power unit over internal combustion. "Engineers admit frankly," said a 1919 ad, "that the gas engine gives only 25 per cent of the power it consumes. The steam auto, being much simpler in construction, operation and care, makes it difficult to understand why the poppet valve engine maintains its supremacy. Certainly not because it is efficient as a power producer."

The Stanleys could still out-accelerate with ease any gasoline auto, even of much greater power, and "they distinguish themselves by the silence and dignity of their behavior. They give passengers a matchless sense of comfort and security." Which was all perfectly true; yet in some perverse way, having hypnotized the public, the giant of internal combustion was inexorably pushing the last of the steamers out of the arena of commercial contest.

The 1921 Stanleys with "Power correctly generated, correctly controlled, correctly applied to the rear wheels," were slicker, smoother, faster and so exactly like a "conventional" auto in appearance that you could hardly tell the one from the other, except for the steamer's "silent behavior." Yet sales continued to drop and steam car lovers were, by then, shrinking into a minor group of "enthusiasts."

Highest priced of 1912 Stanleys was Model 87 Touring Car for seven passengers which sold for $2,500. It filled the demand for a big, powerful car. Used the 4½x6½ in. two-cylinder, 30 hp engine. Its weight was 3,000 pounds.

Mountain wagon; the 1909 Model 88 Steam Station Wagon suited special need of the Loveland-Estes Park Transportation Co. Seated 12 passengers and had two-cylinder 30 hp engine for easy mountain climbing. A bargain at $2,300.

Two-passenger Runabout, Model 62 for 1910, combined a rakish look with good performance. Its engine was a 10 hp job which drove the rear axle direct. At $1,000 it could be bought as shown. Top cost $40. Its weight was 1,400 lbs.

The design of the 1911 Model 73 Steam Touring Car featured a handmade Torpedo type body of aluminum plus fullblown fenders. Weight was around 1,650 pounds. This steamer, complete with top, windshields, etc., cost $1,660.

Model 64, two-passenger 1913 Roadster, used the horizontal, two-cylinder engine of 30 hp. Handmade aluminum body was detachable. In this model the price of $1,200 included all accessories such as top, horn, windshield, speedometer, etc.

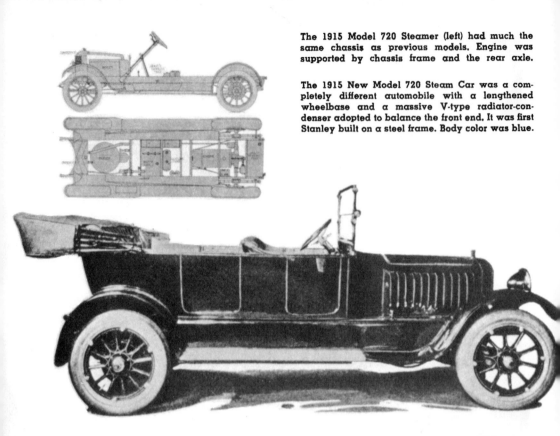

The 1915 Model 720 Steamer (left) had much the same chassis as previous models. Engine was supported by chassis frame and the rear axle.

The 1915 New Model 720 Steam Car was a completely different automobile with a lengthened wheelbase and a massive V-type radiator-condenser adopted to balance the front end. It was first Stanley built on a steel frame. Body color was blue.

The 1914 Model 79 Light Delivery Wagon (below) had quite a vogue. The engine did 420 rpm at 30 mph and the carrying capacity was 1,500 pounds. Price was $1,360 sans body which ran to $600.

In its final attempts to combat the gas engine, a 1923 issue of The Steam Car, a magazine published by the Stanley Motor Carriage Co., resorted to ridicule by giving a dictionary definition of "Clutch": (noun) —"A sudden and violent attempt to seize"; (verb)—"To seize convulsively or eagerly."

The 1923 New Model 740 Stanley Steamer featured "a highly refined and improved chassis offered in five attractive body styles, built closer to the ground on the 130-in. chassis."

But nothing helped any more. The fault lay not with the Stanley but with public taste. There simply were not enough customers to make ends meet. In March 1923, the company was placed in the hands of the receiver, lingering on precariously until February 1924 when S.L.G. Cox of the Steam Vehicle Corp. of America made a cash offer of $500,000 for the plant and assets of the Stanley firm. He also undertook to pay off in full the company's outstanding accounts estimated at $360,000. In return, the purchasers were to take first Preferred Stock. Since the total Stanley assets were valued at $572,204, the receiver accepted the offer.

The Steam Vehicle Corp. of America had already bought out the Steam Bus Syndicate of Chicago, and the new merger, capitalized at half a million dollars, catered to three interests: steam passenger cars, trucks and buses. It was planned to resume the manufacture of Stanley Steamers at once in the Newton plant under the direction of Jacob E. Gremlich, formerly identified with the Watson Truck Corp. of Canastota, N. Y., and the Sandford Motor Truck Co. of Syracuse, N. Y. "New York Steam buses and trucks," said the announcement, "will be manufactured at Canastota by the White Division of the Corporation, so named because it is in charge of Raymond

Stanley 1916 Steam Roadster Model 725 has husky V-type radiator which was useful if not exactly artistic. It condensed exhausted steam to water.

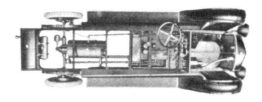

Horizontal engine of Model 725 chassis (below) was geared direct to rear axle thru differential.

Model 726 three-passenger 1916 Roadster was considered very sporty in its day. Two-cylinder, double-acting engine of 20 hp was geared to produce 30 mph at 447 rpm and had only 13 moving parts.

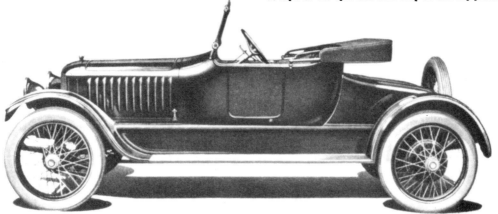

E. White, formerly production manager of the Duesenberg plant, Elizabeth, N. Y. It is proposed to use in the steam trucks and buses the Winslow high-pressure steam boiler developed by the corporation."

Resumed in 1924, the production of the New Stanley Steamer was continued through 1925 with only detail changes which included a shorter (122-in.) wheelbase, a frame lowered by 4-in., hydraulic four-wheel brakes, balloon tires and more streamlined bodywork. The range was reduced to two models and the price of the cheaper Phaeton was cut by about $100. Exhibited at the New York and Chicago International Shows, the New Stanley drew polite attention and curious admiration—but few buyers. It never lived to see the year 1926; nor does anything very sensational appear to have been achieved by the Steam Vehicle Corp. of America.

But nine years later, the magic name of Stanley flared up again with a brilliant burst of light against the somewhat dingy gray of the automotive skies, from which the last traces of color and originality seemed to have vanished.

In 1934 came this announcement: "The organization for active operation of the Stanley Steam Motor Corp. is foreshadowed

Four-passenger 1917 Coupe Model could get under way in one minute. The body was of aluminum and finished in gray and black. Driving compartment (right) shows brake, hook-up pedal and throttle.

A photo of the famous Stanley Twins in their 1917 20 hp Touring Car, "The car your wife can drive."

in an offering of 50,000 shares of participating Class A stock with a par value of $5.00. The new Corporation, organized in Delaware, will be the successor to the Stanley Motor Carriage Co. established 1898 and who have headquarters in Chicago. The new company proposes to manufacture a city steam bus with rear power plant assembly incorporating the advantages of an aerodynamic design. The board of directors includes John H. Brause, formerly the Stanley Co.'s testing engineer, and Elmer G. Knox, formerly production manager of the Yellow Coach Mfg. Co."

Considered hot automotive news in March 1935, was this further release: "With the announcement of the New Stanley Steam Motors Corp. acquiring the name and patents of the parent company, inquiries have been coming in in quantities. This is an indication of the general public interest in steam cars which has maintained at a high level even though none has been manufactured in the last seven years." (Seems they forgot about the Doble.) "In the meantime, a program of research and experimentation has been engaged in and the result has been to develop a Stanley Steamer for which heavy duty bus and truck operation has created

The 1919 Model 735 Coupe had a 20 hp engine which could deliver up to 80 hp. Its weight was 3,560 pounds. The Stanley Company kept plugging the advantages of steam to their dwindling market.

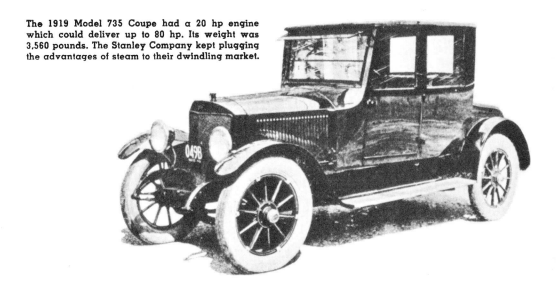

The 1918 Model 736 four-passenger Touring Car could go at 50 mph or 2 mph. It was priced at $2,750.

an economic demand." It never quite did.

Details of the "research and experimentation" read thus: "In the tests, the engine which was of 1908 type built by the original company is said to be capable of developing power equal to a gasoline engine twice the size. The flash-type boiler, thermostatically controlled, is a revision from the old Stanley patents by the use of new materials. Steam exhaust is returned to the boiler through the radiator-condenser. Vibration is said to be minimized due to the fact that no gears or transmission linkage are required. Hydraulic brakes are used on all four wheels, with the body of the bus streamlined and the wheels skirted to lessen wind resistance. The bus has dual rear tires and safety glass throughout. Capacity is 30 passengers. Plans call for a limited production of possibly 150 buses during the first year."

By January 1936, it looked as though things were really getting on the move at last.

"Stanley Steamers are going back into production in the next 90 days," declared Harry W. Gahagan, president of the Stanley Steam Motors Corp., successors to the Stanley Steam Motor Carriage Corp. "No attempt to invade the passenger car field will be made at the outset. Rather, the company will confine its efforts to the bus field initially; later attacking truck problems and then the tractor field. Passenger car engine production will be the last attempted, if at all. Present plans call for a production of two sizes of engines; one for 22 and the other for 44 passenger buses. Both power plants will be of such size as to give a speed of 60 mph at 900 rpm. The new engine will burn low grade fuel and have from 37 to 51 moving parts, depending upon the size of the engine."

According to Mr. Gahagan, the bus installations were to be of the rear-assembly type, "affording great boiler room." He added that "advantage of every metallurgical advancement in recent years has been taken in designing the new engine."

Ninety days went by, and then 90 weeks, and the aging F.O. Stanley must have smiled sadly to himself and shaken his head. Nothing more was heard of the Stanley Steam Motors Corp., and, in fact, the only other news to hit the press in connection with the magic name of Stanley was the passing of Mr. F.O. from a heart ailment on October 3, 1940. •

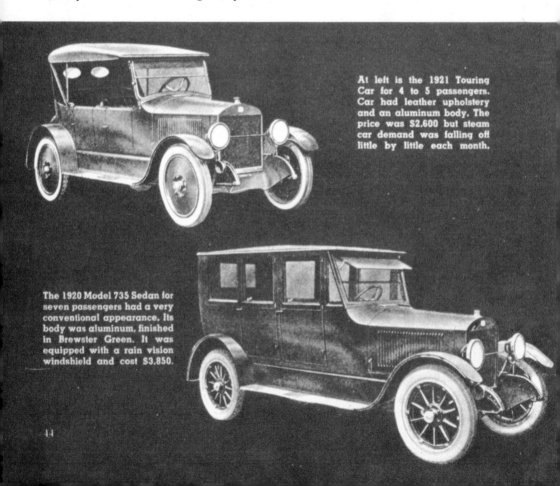

At left is the 1921 Touring Car for 4 to 5 passengers. Car had leather upholstery and an aluminum body. The price was $2,600 but steam car demand was falling off little by little each month.

The 1920 Model 735 Sedan for seven passengers had a very conventional appearance. Its body was aluminum, finished in Brewster Green. It was equipped with a rain vision windshield and cost $3,850.

The new Stanley Model 740 seven-passenger Phaeton produced in 1922 was continued for two years. Brake design was simplified and the rear axle made sturdier. It was fitted with a tailored top and curtains at sides. The price was $2,750.

In 1924 the Stanley Motor Carriage Co. sold out to the Steam Vehicle Corp. of America. It revamped the New Stanley twice and the 1925 model (the last Stanley made) is shown at the right. It tempted few.

In 1935 the Stanley Steam Motors Corp. sprang into life and published this photo of a luxury steam bus based on the patents of the defunct Stanley. The project folded before any buses were produced.

Seen at the finish of the 100 Mile Long Island Endurance Contest, held April 16, 1902, these three White Steamers came through with perfect scores. They gave the crews no trouble at all.

The White

Though surviving only a decade, this Steam Car was second longest lived.

In a ten mile race at Detroit Fair Grounds this "streamlined" but otherwise all stock 1901 White Steamer scored a runaway victory in first racing attempt. Was so far ahead, others were out of sight.

THOUGH THE WHITE STEAM CAR survived only a decade, it was the second longest lived of any passenger steamer ever produced in the U. S., and during its colorful career took part with conspicuous success in more contests of all kinds than any other steamer.

The White, embodiment of an automotive ideal in the mind of Rollin H. White, was introduced in 1901 by the White Sewing Machine Co., Cleveland, Ohio, a firm that had been in business since 1870 and was then the second largest maker of sewing machines in the world. Acclaimed immediately by steam car enthusiasts, the newcomer proved itself by scoring a decisive track victory during its first year of production. The event was a 10-mile race at the Detroit Fair Grounds, Michigan, where a White steamer ran away from all opposition.

September 1902 saw designer Rollin H.

First Steam Carriage produced by White in 1901 by the White Sewing Machine Co., had a two-cylinder, double-acting engine of 6 hp, with link-reversing gear. Claimed "balanced and vibrationless," unit got superheated steam from a flash-tube generator. Copper water tank held 20 gals., enough for 30 miles; gasoline tank held eight gals., enough for 125 miles. Stanhope cost $1,000, weighed 1,100 lbs.

Basic 1902 Stanhope remained much the same, but wheelbase was lengthened by six to 72 in. and a front-mounted condenser now gave the car a more balanced look. Cycle-type fenders added to finish.

White, a sportsman who competed in many events, set five new records for steam vehicles from two to 10 miles at Glenville Track near Cleveland. Upholding US honors abroad, a perfectly standard White Steam Carriage completed a 650-mile Reliability Contest in England with 100 per cent scores, using only 13 quarts of fuel a day. Only two entries in a field of 70 managed a perfect score—the White being one of them. Three more White steamers were awarded Non-Stop Certificates on a 100-mile Endurance Run from New York to Westport and back, organized by the Automobile Club of America. There were 55 starters and 11 non-finishers.

The following year, keeping pace with technical developments, the White featured a compound engine and an 80-in. wheelbase, six inches longer than before. Automatic engine lubrication and two independent sets of brakes also were introduced in a carriage that was bigger, huskier and more powerful. By then, White steamers had won four gold medals, scooped five important races, earned 14 First Class Certificates and set up numerous records in contests of every description.

In 1903 the firm produced its first steam Delivery Wagon, entering the commercial vehicle field with an excellent product. It then had sales agencies in 10 American cities as well as in London, England, where Walter C. White acted as European Representative.

By 1904 the White appeared with its first enclosed passenger bodies, featuring a luxury Limousine among four new models. That year, too, running in a 1,000-mile Reliability Contest over in England, a White steam car covered the distance in eight days, making seven non-stop runs between control points. Tackling a hillclimb which was part of this event, it

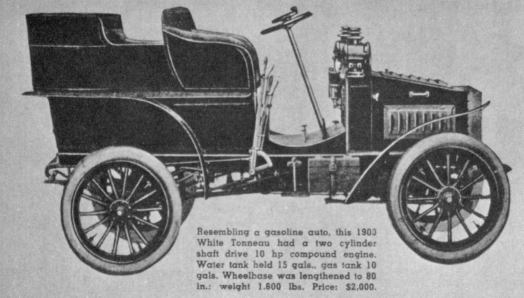

Resembling a gasoline auto, this 1903 White Tonneau had a two cylinder shaft drive 10 hp compound engine. Water tank held 15 gals., gas tank 10 gals. Wheelbase was lengthened to 80 in.; weight 1,600 lbs. Price: $2,000.

Steam Delivery Wagon introduced in 1903 had same specifications as passenger car but used chain drive. Ornamental cab and body housed 500 lb. payload; weighed 1,700 lbs. Speed 30 mph.

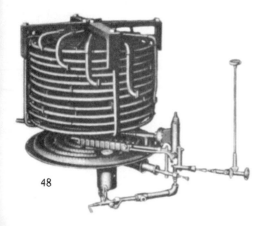

So-called "flash tube generator" of 1904 Whites (shown above with outer case and asbestos packing removed) was in reality a water-tube boiler built in coils over a burner but with this difference: outer end of coils were carried to top. This prevented water from running down, displacing steam.

scaled a grade 3,960 ft. long, averaging 8.5 per cent, at a speed of 13.63 mph.

With the 1905 appearance of the underslung racing White steamer "Whistling Billy," driver Webb Jay began to make gasoline-powered cars look sick. Early in July he scored an easy win over a 90-hp Fiat and a 60-hp Thomas at Morris Park Track, New York, covering a mile in 48⅘ secs.

By then, production of White steamers had moved up into the 2,500-to-3,000-pound weight class and become full-sized automobiles offering passenger comfort equal to that of many costlier gasoline autos. A 15-hp engine was now standard equipment and there were various detail improvements such as dual water pumps and a foot-operated "constant positive clutch" that allowed the engine to run free when the car was stopped. The firm was awarded a Grand Prize at the 1905 Louisiana Purchase Exposition and at the World's Fair in St. Louis, Missouri. Rollin H. White also earned a gold medal for "conspicuous inventive skill in developing the steam car." Meanwhile, at the annual Eagle Rock Hillclimb held in New Jersey, Webb Jay's "Whistling Billy"—so named because of its high-pitched exhaust note—put up an amazing performance with a time only

The chassis of the 1905 White steamer had front-mounted vertical engine and stern boiler in unit with the water tank. Front condenser gave hood a "conventional" look. F.o.b. Cleveland was $2,000.

Model "D" of 1904 was first White Steam Limousine. A two-cylinder compound engine, 3 and 5 x 3½ in., with Stephenson link valve motion providing the power. Was highest priced of four cars at $2,700.

3⅗ secs. slower than a gas-powered Renault of four times its horsepower and price. It was only one second slower than a 90-hp Fiat costing $16,000. Jay went on to capture the World's Mile Track Record with "Whistling Billy" at 74.07 mph and won more honors at race meets in Nashville, Tenn. Detroit, Mich., and Cleveland. "Thus," said the White company, "the notion cherished in some quarters that the gasoline car was assured of supremacy on the track at least, has taken its place with many other discarded superstitions about steamers." Slightly miffed, "Horseless Age" magazine ran a pointed editorial about the "Decadence of Track Racing," and held that "the legitimate manufacturer may be beaten by some home made racing freak . . . valueless to the industry."

White enthusiasts merely smiled. That year, during the first Glidden Tour held over 866 miles of tricky roads and climbs, no less than 10 White steamers were included among the 44 entries, and the majority of these figured among the 26 finishers who gained awards. In every annual Glidden Tour thereafter, until 1910, White steam cars showed up to advantage against their gasoline rivals. Just to prove the point, a White set a new record on July 28 and 29, 1905, carrying four passengers

Here seen at Morris Park Track, New York, July 4, 1905, Webb Jay runs away from Chevrolet, Sartori and Roberts. Their Fiats and Thomas were no match for Webb's White Steam "Whistling Billy."

Covered wagon appearance was achieved by cape top and side curtains on the Model "F" Touring Car, new in 1906. This 18 hp two-cylinder compound engine had Stephenson link motion, four sets of eccentrics. Flash-tube generator built 275 psi working steam pressure. $2,950 with curtains.

and luggage over the 470 mountainous miles between San Francisco and Los Angeles, California. This, too, was the year when the White Sewing Machine Co. changed its name to the White Co., and channeled the manufacture of sewing machines into a separate enterprise.

For 1906, the White Steamer's compound engine was stepped up to 18 hp and the boiler came in for some authoritative praise. Professor Thurston, Dean of the School of Mechanical Engineering at Cornell University, said in a professional report: "The construction of the White generator permits insurance of safety against pressures of excessive amount, since these small tubes are strong enough to withstand enormous pressures—pressures, in fact, many times greater than those employed." To which the company added: "Our standard has always been to build a car able to surmount any road conditions which might be encountered." It also adopted the motto: "The Incomparable White—the Car for Service," reminding the public that "White cars now offered have behind them a record of five years of successful service. By this time 1,500

The White Standard Steam Touring Car of 1905 was equipped with a two cylinder compound engine of 15 hp. The "flash-tube" boiler built steam to 350 psi from 17-gallon water tank, 15 gallons of gasoline. Weight 2,433 lbs., price: $2,500.

White steamers had been built and sold, "twice as many large touring cars as were made by any other manufacturer in the world."

In May 1906, just to keep the ball rolling, Webb Jay with "Whistling Billy" scored several more victories against all comers at Belmont Park track.

Power on the 1907 Whites was again stepped up to 20 and 30 hp, and steam pressure boosted to 600 pounds. "Certain noteworthy improvements along the lines of White progress" included a flow regulator providing "constant steam pressure at a constant degree of superheat under all conditions." But prices were up as well, and the seven model range now had a high of $4,700. Starting with President Theodore Roosevelt, notable people in all walks of life and countless sporting personalities such as Ezra Fitch, founder of Abercrombie and Fitch, owned White steamers. That year, at the Wilkes-Barre Hillclimb, Pa., held on Decoration Day, Walter C. White set up a new record, beating by a wide margin the best time of any gasoline-powered auto. So great was the inrush of business that the White company opened

Leather upholstered folding double seats for owners desiring "—a seating capacity greater than that which the car ordinarily affords—" were available on the 1906 Model "F" for an additional $40. When not in use, extra seats folded down.

Describing equipment of the 1906 Model "F," White catalogue stated: "—acetylene headlights are not included in prices for each style of car." Recommended were these Parabolens Solar lamps supplied from Prest-o-lite tank mounted on side.

This 1907 Model "G" was a luxury job with seven passenger capacity, sold for $3,700 (cape top was extra) in a range from $3,400 to $3,700. Tanks held 17 gallons of water, 24 of gasoline. Car weighed 2,800 lbs. A 20 hp Model "H" sold for $2,400.00.

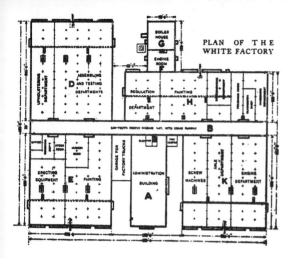

New factory building completed in 1907 to cope with the world-wide rush of orders for White cars centered all production under one roof, from a blacksmith shop to an upholstering department. Plant was located on a 30 acre site in Cleveland.

a new factory on a 30-acre site near Cleveland to cope with orders from all over the world. At a time when millions of motorists seemed irrevocably to have adopted the gasoline automobile, this plant and that of the Stanley brothers were the two remaining oases for steam car devotees.

Whites reached peak power and size in 1908 and 1909 with the 40-hp Model "M" steamer built on a 122-in. wheelbase; but by then the firm's competition activities had tapered off sharply and the initial advantages in performance and simplicity of the steamer over the gas car seemed to be forgotten. In 1908, however, a White made a clean sweep of the San Francisco Hillclimb held in conjunction with the Automobile Show, crossing the line 16 secs. faster than its nearest gasoline competitor. It was also during this period that a factory-entered White steam racer won the Model Road Race between Denver and Brighton, Colorado; but the "conventional" internal combustion automobile had,

The huge chassis assembly room of the White factory included a Testing Rack (top photo below) where six to ten chassis at a time had boilers, engines and other components subjected to a thorough going over before bodies were mounted. The inverted funnels were used to duct out combustion fumes.

Improvements on the 1908 Model "H" included hike of 225 psi pressure over Model "F" (a big jump) while weight was reduced to around 2,150 pounds. Costing $2,500, above model had new pilot light.

President Theodore Roosevelt (hand on hat, above) personally owned and liked this 1907 Model "G." White Steam Cars were used as official White House vehicles, only steam cars thus honored.

The Model "G" chassis, shown below with a light racing body, made a sensational hill climb in Wilkes Barre, Pa., on Decoration Day, 1907. Driven by Walter G. White, it set new record, going up in 1 min. 49⅘ sec., winning by full ten seconds.

through the birth of gigantic manufacturing enterprises, quantity production and low prices, so consolidated its position that the die was cast.

In 1910, the White Co. bravely announced: "The White Steam Car is now entering its tenth year before the public. No other make of car numbers among its users so many personages prominent in public life, and no other car is in demand in so many countries. The unequaled hill climbing ability of the White, its superior adaptability for traveling over rough and sandy roads, and its low cost upkeep are other factors that have contributed toward its increasing popularity. The advance in the 1910 models is that kerosene may be used as fuel instead of gasoline."

To prove the point, a White steamer completed the grueling 1910 Glidden Tour of 2,650 miles on kerosene alone, without loss of a single point.

But if this courageous firm seemed to be whistling in the dark, it knew well enough what the new dawn must inevitably bring. Accordingly, it was formulating plans to ensure its survival. The year 1910 was the last one for White Steam Cars. With the closing of this century's first decade, the company began producing gasoline autos, and to this day lives on in the commercial field, a very successful enterprise. •

53

Driver's compartment on the 1909 White Steam cars had all the gadgets and gauges dear to the enthusiast: AA —Air Pump; 109—Crank-case Oiler Pump; 108—Cylinder Hand Oiler; 209—Air Gauge; 210—Steam Gauge; 43—Lever for Cylinder Relief Cocks; 42—Pyrometer; 93—Starting Pedal; 91—Cut-Off; 82—Cut-Off Pedal Adjusting Pin; 94—Air Pump Valve Pedal; 95—Brake Pedal.

Built on an "armored wood" chassis frame with a 122 inch wheelbase, the 1909 Model "M" White Steamer reached peak power and size. For the first time in nine years the compound engine varied in more than bore and stroke. It was a lighter two-cylinder unit with fewer parts, using Joy valve motion direct from connecting rods. The "M" Steam Touring Car sold for $4,000, but a smaller companion model known as the "O" with a 104 inch wheelbase sold for $2,000 with full equipment.

Last of the Famous White Steamers were the 1910 "MM" and "OO," basically similar except for size and power. The "OO" is shown above, the "MM" below. Both had two-cylinder compound vertical engines; "MM" of 40 hp with cylinders 3 and 5 by 4¼ inches, "OO" of 20 hp with 2½ and 4¼ by 3 inches. Same "flash tube generator" supplied 600 psi of working steam for both, with kerosene as common fuel.

The "MM" shown here had a Pullman body, seating seven. It had a 17½ gallon water tank against the 13 gallon tank of the "OO." The $4,000 price tag included acetylene headlamps and tank, oil side lamps, horn and tool kit. Seven body styles were available with a high of $5,000. Cape top extra.

Equally at home overseas was the 1902 Locomobile Style 0003 Steam Carriage here seen on the Island of Java. This model carried 32 gallons of water to five of gas for a weight of 1,080 pounds and featured a design that "holds all records for mountain climbing." Price: $950.

The Locomobile

The Locomobile, a Stanley offspring, was a "Siamese twin" to the Mobile.

THE STORY OF the Locomobile steamer ties in closely with that of the Stanley and Mobile steam cars, this machine being the offspring of the former and the "Siamese twin" of the latter. The idea for the Locomobile first originated when A. Lorenzo Barber purchased an early Stanley Steamer in 1897. He was so impressed with it that he decided to enter the field of steam car production which was just then beginning to blossom forth. In partnership with J. B. Walker, formerly of Cosmopolitan Magazine, Barber formed the Automobile Co. of America, incorporated in West Virginia June 17, 1899, with the object of purchasing the Stanley Steamer patents for $250,000, together with the Kingsland property in Tarrytown, New York, where the Stanley was already in production and doing a profitable business. F. E. and F. O. Stanley agreed to the sale.

Almost as soon as the new company was formed, however, some disagreement arose between Barber and Walker. As a result, the following announcement appeared on July 19, 1899: "A. Lorenzo Barber and J. B. Walker, organizers of the Locomobile Co. of America, have made a partition and the outgrowth is two companies. Barber will retain the Locomobile Co. and will manufacture Stanley Carriages. Walker has taken the Mobile Co. of America and will manufacture

Layout of the typical 1900 chassis: simple, practical and compact. Fuel tank was located in front, vertical engine amidships, close to the boiler which in turn dovetailed into water tank.

This was the Locosurrey Stanhope Model No. 5 that was so popular in 1900. Its two-cylinder 10 hp vertical engine, mounted in the back, would run smoothly to 2,000 rpm. Price $1,200.

Stanley Steam Vehicles. The Stanley brothers will act as general managers for both companies for a year."

Barber moved his factory to Bridgeport, Conn., while Walker retained the Kingsland Point plant; but though Locomobile quickly became the best seller among contemporary steamers, neither firm was fated to survive in the steam car battle. After a rather futile spate of direct competition which lasted more than four years and was obviously of benefit to neither, both quit building steamers in 1903; but whereas Walker's Mobile disappeared from the scene for good, Barber's Locomobile was saved by Andrew L. Riker (of Riker Electric fame) who had joined the Locomobile Co. in 1902 and became its vice president and chief engineer.

Realizing where the future lay, Riker immediately went to work designing and developing a gasoline car. This appeared a year later as the "King of the Belgians" model and was first exhibited at the Madison Square Garden Auto Show in New York where it aroused much favorable comment and attracted several buyers. From this gasoline forerunner, the Locomobile was destined to develop into one of the finest and greatest of all American cars and to remain one of the Industry's leaders in the luxury class, right on until 1929. •

Short wheelbase emphasized the skinny, high-perched look of this 1901 Style No. 3 Locomobile, below. It had the same specifications as the previous year's models but weighed only 800 pounds. One of eight styles ranging from $750 to $1,400, it sold for $900 with the top.

Cut-away, above, of the 1901 Style No. 2 Steam Buggy showed the "Stanley System" of propulsion with all the working parts snugly tucked inside the body, including the vertical boiler and engine. Weight was 850 pounds including 21 gallons of water, five of gas. Lowest priced: $750.

Huskier, heavier and more powerful, the 1903 Dos-a-Dos appeared in Locomobile's last year of steam car manufacture. With 33 gallons of water and two of gas weight came to 1,500 pounds. It sold for $1,600, highest priced in a range reduced to four models. Steamers were discontinued.

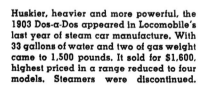

58

The
Steam Car
Album

An album of the more important
Steam Cars in picture and text
from the year 1860 through 1929.

American

FIRST AMERICAN Steam Phaeton, above, was completed June 10, 1922, and shown at the Chicago Pageant of Progress held on the Municipal Pier, August that year. It had a two-cylinder, compound, double-acting engine with piston valves, Joy valve gear and only 17 moving parts. The water-tube boiler, tested to 4,000 pounds (cold water) pressure provided a steam pressure of 500 to 600 pounds. Water and fuel tanks (kerosene) held 25 gallons each, and the car did 30 mph at 500 rpm. Maximum speed was 65 mph with a 250-mile cruising range. The engine ran 10,000 miles on three quarts of oil.

Initial production schedule called for 100 cars. The firm had already produced its first steam truck six weeks earlier. "With dealer contracts totaling $300,000 for exclusive territories," said President R. R. Howard, "the company expects a revenue of $2,000,000." One model only was offered at $1,650, but despite conventional looks and handsome Lincoln-type "radiator," the American flopped. An improved burner and boiler featured for 1923, together with a choice of roadster, sedan and coupe bodies, didn't save the firm from bankruptcy in 1924, after a span of only three years. Builders were the American Steam Truck Co., Elgin, Ill.

Conventional layout of American Steamer chassis (top right, page 61), featured boiler and engine under hood; shaft drive to rear axle; water tank under driving seat and fuel tank at rear. "Radiator" was steam condenser, but transmission was eliminated.

In the panel (top left, page 61), we see: upper left, the burner of the American Steamer; right, the compact two-cylinder engine; lower left, tubular boiler (provided 50 sq. ft. heating area); right, sectional view of water pump.

Prototype of American Steamer (bottom, page 61), built in 1918, underwent 25 months of rigorous testing and covered 30,000 miles under every road condition to locate weaknesses before design was "frozen." It deserved a better fate. •

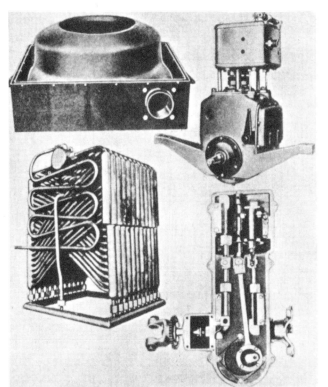

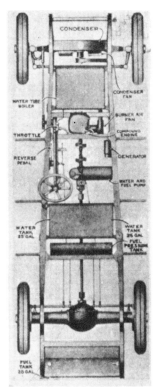

THIS 1898 American Waltham Steam Buggy, manufactured by the
builders of the "Comet" bicycle, was a lightweight job with a
two-cylinder engine, 2½x5-in. set "quarter stroke." The boiler, made
up of 280 tubes, combined an auxiliary water tank to maintain the
required level. A 100-pound working steam pressure could be raised
in five minutes. Water and "gasolene" tanks, located under the floorboards, held 12 and five gallons respectively; weight complete was
500 pounds. This machine was sometimes confused with the Waltham
Steam Buggy, built by the Waltham Manufacturing Company, makers
of the "Orient" bicycle. In those days, three local-built steamers
were seen on the streets of Waltham, a "suburban city" 10 miles west
of Boston. The third vehicle, "nearly ready for production" was the
New England Steam Carriage which appeared a year later. The
American Waltham Manufacturing Company, Waltham, Mass.,
stopped making steamers in 1899, after only two years on the market. •

Amoskeag

BELCHING GREAT CLOUDS of steam and smoke, "Jumbo"—one of the steam fire engines used by the city of Hartford, Conn.—made an impressive sight as it sped to a fire. Ordered in 1889, it was the largest fire-fighting machine in the world. Starting in 1876, Hartford renewed orders for steam-powered Amoskeag Automobile Fire Engines in 1879, 1889 and 1901. Prototype, built by P. R. Hodge of New York in 1840, had a two-cylinder, horizontal engine and resembled a locomotive but weighed only 3,000 pounds. It was quite successful.

Ornate as a child's toy, the 1901 Amoskeag Automobile Fire Engine (above) was a powerful steamer with a two-cylinder, 9½x8-in. reversible engine that put out 100 hp. Its upright seamless copper tube boiler consisted of 313 tubes that generated 120 pounds of steam. Of the "submerged flue" type, it was 40-in. in diameter. The water tank held 100 gallons and cannel coal was used for fuel. Despite its hulking weight of 17,000 pounds, the Amoskeag would do 25 mph and climb grades "as any horse-drawn fire engine." The rear wheels were chain-driven and equipment included a pump "which can throw 1,450 gallons of water per minute a distance of 348 ft. through 50 ft. of leading hose." Steering was by a 36-in. hand-wheel located up front. Cost of maintenance was claimed to be $28 per month, compared with $62 for a horse-drawn fire engine.

Formed in 1867, the Amoskeag Corporation of Manchester, N. H., became the Manchester Locomotive Works at the turn of the century. First fire engine built by this firm was used in the great fire of Boston in 1872, while the next four were purchased by the city of New York between 1868 and 1870, though New York didn't favor steam fire engines "for various reasons." In 1873, Detroit ordered one of these machines which proved a success, even though the makers themselves were "somewhat sceptical" about the new compound engine installed. The Amoskeag was the longest lived steamer of all, from 1876 to 1906. •

Baker

IN AUGUST 1926, Dr. A. O. Baker, long associated with steam car research in the U. S., announced a new steam-driven motor bus "expected to set trade records in cutting fuel and lubrication costs." The engine was a five-cylinder rotary job 4¼x3½ in. that developed 85 to 90 hp at 1,600 rpm and put out 1,800 ft. lbs. of torque at stalling load.

The tubular boiler gave a working steam pressure of 600 psi and was pressure fed from a 30-gallon tank. Gasoline was fed to the burner from a 40-gallon tank by two Autopulse electric pumps. Weighing 7,800 pounds, this handsome, low-slung steam coach had a 235-in. wheelbase and would do 45 mph at 1,200 rpm. Maximum speed was 50 mph.

Features included Lockheed hydraulic four-wheel brakes; a conventional foot throttle and Goodrich special oval balloon tires: 35x6x7 in. Price with single deck body was $10,000, but chassis was equally adaptable for a double-decker. Despite numerous advantages, this fine steamer made no impression on noisy gasoline rivals. Prejudice rather than price tag was the cause of failure. Production span lasted only two years, ending in 1928.

Considerable secrecy guarded extensive tests of the original Baker Steam Coach chassis (below) which had its boiler under the hood. The engine was located in place of conventional clutch housing and propelled the drive shaft direct, doing away with the need of any transmission. The chassis (see truck chassis, top of page 65) had massive cross members. Firm also built a steam tractor with similar layout. shorter wheelbase. Engine was lubricated by a mixture of oil, kerosene and graphite. Compact, efficient and completely enclosed.

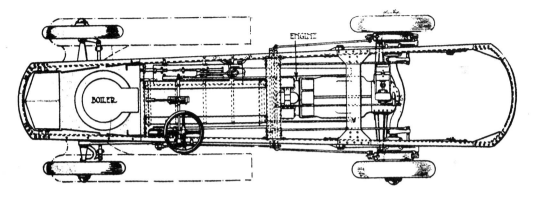

Top view (above) of Dr. Baker's Steam Truck which featured a two-cylinder, slide-valve "uniflow" engine.

the engine was built around a central drive shaft and had a displacement of 248 cu. in. It was a real engineering job, far ahead of other steam designs.

In 1921, automotive engineers took a good look at Dr. Baker's Steam Truck (see diagrams above and below) which featured a two-cylinder, slide-valve engine of "uni-flo" principle, for which a 23 per cent efficiency increase was claimed over steam engines of corresponding size. Output was 39.3 hp at 1,200 rpm. The boiler consisted of cold-drawn steel tubing coils tested to 4,000 psi, and working steam pressure could be raised from 100 to 500 psi in 20 or 35 seconds, or from 200 to 500 psi in 12 to 17 seconds. Time taken to raise steam from

cold was not stated, but the burner was so designed that gasoline, alcohol, paraffin distillate, crude oils or any mixture of these could be used for fuel. The engine drove the rear axle direct, through a gearing device which embodied a free wheel. The truck's payload was two tons.

In November 1925, Dr. Baker built a new steam car and invited newsmen to take a ride. It was their first trip in a Cleveland-built steamer since the White Company had stopped making steam cars in 1910. First known as Baker Motors, Inc., Cleveland, Ohio, the firm later took the name of an affiliated concern—the Steam Appliance Corporation of America, Inc. It lasted from 1921 to 1928. •

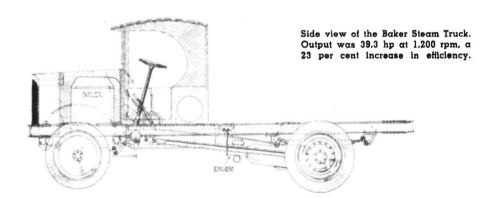

Side view of the Baker Steam Truck. Output was 39.3 hp at 1,200 rpm, a 23 per cent increase in efficiency.

Binney & Burnham

THIS 1902 Steam Runabout "as recently delivered to Elliott C. Lee, vice-president of the Massachusetts Automobile Club" mounted a two-cylinder, slide valve, link motion engine of 2½x3½ in. bore and stroke. A 17-in. water-tube boiler working at 150 psi supplied steam. Water and gas were carried in pressed steel tanks with a capacity of 48 and 14 gallons respectively. Weight was 1,100 pounds. Maker claimed, "It climbs steep grades at a very fast pace and will stand much abuse on hard roads."

Two models were available (with or without folding front seat) featuring "a burner of special design; inclosed differential, double-acting handbrake and McNutt steering gear." The 3½-in. tires on 30-in. wood wheels were made by the New York Vehicle Company. Note steering wheel. •

EXCELLENT FINISH was a feature of the 1903 Boss Steam Carriage, of which its makers claimed: "Once started with a match—ready for the whole day." It had a two-cylinder, seven hp engine fed from a 17 in. boiler with 525 tubes tested to 700 psi (cold water). Working steam was 150 pounds. Water tank held 35 gallons and the fuel container (gasoline or kerosene) provided 15 gallons or enough for 150 to 200 miles. Burner pilot light kept up a constant head of steam for a quick start, and the 30-in. wood wheels ran on three-inch clincher tires. Body was hand-made, upholstered in fine quality leather and given 17 coats of paint.

"Not one mile of railroad or street railways is driven by gas power in the whole U. S.," said maker. "Why? Because it is not reliable!"

Advertised "a model of simplicity, safety, durability and comfort," the Boss steamer was offered at $1,000 and weighed 1,300 pounds. It was built by the Boss Knitting Machine Works, Reading, Pa., from 1903 to 1907. Running gear of the 1903 Boss Steam Carriage was mounted on a light, rigid sub-frame (shown directly above) independent of body which rode on carriage springs. An easy ride resulted. •

67

Brecht

BUILT by one of nine new steam car firms to appear in 1902, this 1904 Brecht Steam Stanhope was already at the end of a brief existence. Power was supplied by a two-cylinder, vertical, double-acting reversible engine of five hp at 450 rpm. The boiler held 402 copper tubes with a heating area of 60 sq. ft. and a working steam pressure of 210 psi. It was tested to 1,000 psi (cold water) and fitted with a fusible plug to prevent burst tubes. Water and gas tanks held 38 and 7½ gallons and the weight was 1,100 pounds. The Brecht Automobile Company of St. Louis, Mis-

souri, built both steam and electric machines, "entirely practical, keeping abreast of rapid development in auto construction." It also offered running gear and bodies suitable for "various steam and electric engines." Dos-a-Dos here shown cost $1,240 and was one of four models with a price range of $1,060 to $1,775, but by 1904 (despite tempting discounts of up to 50 per cent on India tires) the firm was forced to sell out. Purchasers of complete stock, tools, machinery and good will were H. F. Borbein & Company, who promptly held a half-price sale to clear "many steam and electric vehicles." New owners quit building cars and supplied only parts and running gear. They survived until 1908.

The Brecht Fancy Steam Delivery Wagon, seen at left, seemed to lack only a horse, but this 1904 model didn't need one. It had a larger (12 hp) engine than the passenger cars, but the same boiler. Carried were 67 gallons of water and 25 of gasoline—enough for a day's run. Weight, with full tanks, was 2,600 pounds and the payload 1,800 pounds. At 10 to 15 mph, operating cost was two cents per mile. Price, complete, $1,775. Discontinued 1904. •

Brooks

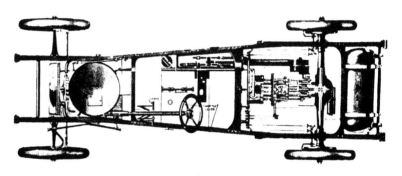

THOUGH CANADIAN, the 1924 Brooks Steamer—one of the last few makes of steam cars ever to appear—reflected American influence both in design and looks. Its two-cylinder, 4x4½ in. horizontal slide-valve engine had detachable heads and the 20 in. vertical fire-tube boiler derived water from a 21 gallon copper tank, producing enough steam for 450 to 500 miles. Gas capacity was 15 gallons—a 225 to 300 mile supply; kerb weight 3,800 pounds. Said the makers: "The engine gives four steady power impulses per revolution, an equal number to that of an eight-cylinder internal combustion engine. Getaway is smoother and much quicker, with a greater tire mileage." The fabric sedan body was made to Brooks design by the American Auto Trimming Co., Walkerville, Ontario, and was remarkable for "a total absence of rumbling and vibration, squeaks and rattles." It was "a revelation and a delight." Lone model offered sold for $2,000, but the buyer had a choice of three wheelbases; 112, 122 and 132 inch. Founded in August 1923 with a capital of $5,000,000, Brooks Steam Motors, Ltd., produced their first car in December 1923 and gave up in 1930.

Simplicity was a feature of the 1924 Brooks Steamer chassis which had boiler housed under hood and an engine with only 38 moving parts, driving the rear axle direct. This in turn drove the generator for current supply. Gas tank was rear-slung and water tank was located below driving seat. •

Capitol

JUSTIFYING ITS NAME in appearance if not in performance, the 1902 Capitol Chariot was one of many steamers that failed to make the grade. Powered by a two-cylinder, double-acting engine, 2¾x3¾ in., it put forth six hp through a chain drive to the rear axle. Boiler held 420 tubes and featured a "dry steam dome." Working steam pressure was 160 psi, supplied from a 34 gallon water tank. Eight gallons of "gasolene" were carried and the machine scaled 1,200 pounds, ready to go. The Kelly burner, wood wheels and solid rubber tires were conventional enough, but seating arrangement anticipated modern ideas by allowing enough room for three abreast. Fourth passenger rode backwards, facing the others. Offered in one model priced at $1,200 and built by the Capitol Auto Company, Washington, D. C., this machine was on the market for only a year. •

Century

INCLINED shaft drive to the rear axle by "chainless bevel gear" was an unusual feature on this 1901 No. 1 Century Steam Vehicle. Engine was a two-cylinder, vertical, marine type job of 4¾ hp, deriving 175 psi of steam pressure from a water tube boiler tested to 700 psi—enough to maintain a "steady 25 mph." Weight, excluding 34 gallons of water and 10 of gas was 750 pounds. Claimed to be of "ample strength and durability," the Century had double-shoe brakes and a burner pilot light for quick starts. It competed in the New York-Buffalo Endurance run without losing any points. Price (with Victoria top) was $950. Production by the Century Motor Vehicle Company, Syracuse, N. Y., lasted from 1899 through 1902. In 1903 the firm began making a "Tourist Gasoline Car."

The crankshaft of the 1901 Century steamer (right) was forged from a solid billet, machined into finished article. •

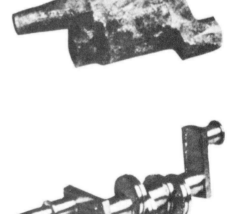

Clark

IN ITS FINAL year of production was this Model LXX Clark Steamer of 1909. Four-cylinder, 3¼x3½ in. horizontal opposed engine carried under frame was of "simple condensing" type and developed 20 hp. Flash boiler had a working pressure of 750 psi, which was unusually high. Twenty gallons of gas supplied the heat. Complete with rakish fenders and tonneau body seating four, this job scaled 1,850 pounds. An unusual feature for a steamer was a two-speed, sliding gear transmission which relayed power through a drive shaft to a floating rear axle. Front axle was tubular for strength and lightness. Offered at $2,750, the LXX was the costlier of two models starting at $2,500. Firm built steamers for 15 years.

Fighting a forlorn rear-guard battle after the decisive defeat of road steam, the Clark Steam Car of 1905 (opposite page, top) contrived to look very much like its gas-powered rivals. Engine was a horizontal, double-opposed, four-cylinder job (mounted amidships) that produced 20 hp for a bore and stroke of 2½x3½ in. The flash boiler, located under the hood, consisted of 360 copper tubes and built a working steam pressure of 150 psi. Tanks held 25 gallons of water and 18 gallons of gas; weight was 2,600 pounds. Claimed "speedy, strong, stylish and easy to manipulate," the Clark offered "accessibility and freedom from repairs." Included was a clutch, designed to allow the engine to run free. Final drive was by bevel gear, and the steering wheel "of novel construction" could be "thrown into a vertical position, making the seat of the operator of the car accessible." Another claim for this seven-passenger job priced at $5,000 was that the weight was "evenly distributed on the wheels, relieving the tires of all undue strain and wear." With canopy top (not shown), price was $300 extra. Edward S. Clark Steam Automobiles, founded in Boston in 1895, moved to Dorchester, Mass., at the turn of the century and remained in business until 1909. •

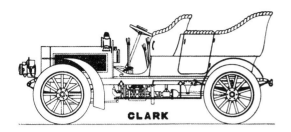

The 1905 Clark Steam Car, fighting a forlorn rear-guard battle after the decisive defeat of road steam, contrived to look like its gas-powered rivals.

CLARK

Cloughley

THIS SHORT-LIVED 1903 Steam Surrey, seating four, featured a two-cylinder, eight hp, slide-valve encased engine mounted in front. A 19 in. water tube boiler provided 175 psi of steam and water was derived from a 25 gallon tank. With enough (gasoline) fuel for 150 miles, weight was 1,450 pounds. Features included a special condenser, wheel or lever steering, 30 in. wheels with three-inch New York B & P tires, and a chain-driven solid live rear axle with ball-bearing differential. The Cloughley Motor Vehicle Company, Parsons, Kansas, offered its steamer in one model only at $1,200 but played it safe by also building an identical gas-powered Surrey. Despite this, the firm survived only two years—1902-1903. •

Coats

THIS 1923 Coats Steam Car entered the market with a flourish of optimism and appeared to hold out great promise which, unfortunately, was not fulfilled. Unusual motive power was the three-cylinder, V-type, 120° single-acting engine, featuring poppet valves and a camshaft. Of 3⅛x4 in. bore and stroke, it had a four-bearing crankshaft and an output of 35 hp. It was located "where the transmission normally is." The boiler, of semi-flash type, had a high working pressure of 600 psi and could produce a full head of steam in 60 seconds. The five gallon water tank sufficed for 300 miles, and fuel capacity was 18 gallons of kerosene. Scaling 2,250 pounds, this steam touring car with a 112 in. wheelbase claimed "remarkable pick-up and smoothness of operation, together with a hill-climbing capacity far ahead of any gas car of equal rated power." Inventor George A. Coats (here seen with Mary Katherine Campbell, Buckeye Beauty who was chosen Miss America) said of his car: "It cuts fuel and maintenance costs in two and doubles tire mileage. There is no gearshift, no pilot light." He also reminded people that "steam has done 90.4 per cent of the world's work requiring power." A convincing argument, supported by a glowing letter from Professor C. A. Norman, Professor of Machine Design at Ohio State University, who in September 1922 tested the Coats steam engine. This interesting power unit had no flywheel but featured a control which, when desired, allowed steam to enter the cylinders "for the full length of the stroke, giving more power." Two body styles—a touring car and three-passenger roadster—were offered at $1,085, and prospects seemed unusually bright. Wisconsin Steamers, Inc., Milwaukee, Wis., an independent dealership organized to handle the Coats, stated: "There is an immediate sale for 300 cars in the city of Milwaukee alone. Before showing your little steamer here, we felt that 800 cars next year would be plenty. Now we want you to consider allotting us in 1923, 1,200 to 1,500 automobiles." But it was all in vain. Founded in May 1922, the plant was sold by January 1924. •

Coldwell

THIS COMPLICATED and impressive Steam Lawn Mower was something of a novelty when it appeared in 1903. The engine was a two-cylinder, slide-valve, reversible job that put forth eight hp, the vertical tubular boiler providing working steam at 180 psi. Gas consumption was 1 to 1½ gallons an hour for a weight of 3,000 pounds. Claimed the maker: "Men and horses are displaced by this machine which will climb a 20 per cent grade and run forward or backward." Although no bargain at $3,000, the Coldwell Steam Mower could easily be converted into a steam roller or a stationary engine. It was originally designed to cut the grass on the grounds of the U. S. Capitol at Washington —a 52-acre expanse with some 30 acres of lawn, "said to be the largest in the world." Despite this, the Coldwell Lawn Mower Company, Newburgh, New York, folded in 1905 after only three years of production. •

Conrad

FAR FROM ORIGINAL in appearance was this 1903 Steam Model 65 Special, powered by a two-cylinder, six hp engine located amidships under the frame and "enclosed in a metal hood." A 20 in. boiler (at rear) produced super-heated steam from 650 copper tubes at 160 psi, water being stored in a 35 gallon tank. Eight gallons of gasoline fed the burner which had a patented pilot light to keep up a head of steam. Weight of this buggy was 1,004 pounds with a two-passenger panel back seat body and full tanks. One of four models (two of them commercial vehicles) with a price range of $800 to $2,500, this one brought $850.

During Christmas 1901, a large Conrad delivery wagon ran for a week making deliveries for a large Buffalo department store. It did the work of three horse-drawn vehicles without trouble. A similar wagon carried mail from the main post office in Buffalo to the Pan American Exposition. Incorporated in Buffalo, April 1900, with a capital stock of $25,000, the Conrad Motor Carriage Company, Buffalo, N. Y., also began manufacturing gasoline cars in 1902, but failed July 1903 and was declared bankrupt a month later. •

Cotta

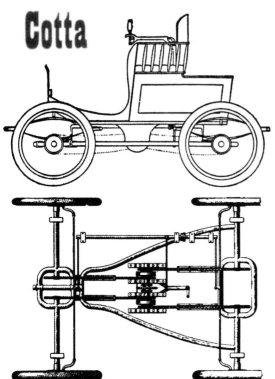

THE 1901 Cotta Steam Vehicle was distinctly unusual in that it featured not only four-wheel drive but also four-wheel steering. Engine was a vertical two-cylinder, six hp job of 2⅞x3¾ in. bore and stroke which derived steam at 180 psi. from a boiler with 406 copper tubes. From a cold start, five minutes were needed to get up a working pressure. Water and gas tanks held 21 and seven gallons and the machine weighed 950 pounds. "Each wheel is independent of the others," said the maker, "and this device causes each wheel to do its share of propelling and to bear its share of wear. Traveling over rough roads is facilitated." The Cotta came in one model which sold for $850 and was built by the Cotta Automobile Company, Lanark, Ill. Production span: 1901-1903.

Chassis of 1901 Cotta Steam Vehicle showed how power was transmitted from a centrally mounted engine to all four wheels by quadruple compensating chain gear. Steering linkage was so arranged that one movement of the tiller caused all four wheels to move on ball joints. Frame was a light tubular welded structure of advanced design for its time. •

Coulthard

IN EVERY SENSE a tough chore horse, the 1905 Coulthard Steam Truck was powered by a big two-cylinder, slide-valve, horizontal engine of 30 hp. The fire-tube boiler (at front) was made up of copper tubes and produced a working steam pressure of 200 psi. Using coal or coke for fuel, this six-ton truck could haul a full load at a steady six mph. Following a gold medal award by the Automobile Club of America, the maker claimed: "Our vehicle carried the greatest load, covered the greatest number of ton-miles, carried the greatest paying load in relation to tare weight and cost less per ton mile than any other vehicle in its class."

A chart was drawn, showing how the Coulthard Truck, with its two-speed sliding gear transmission, chain drive and steel tires, could do the work of two wagons and six horses at a saving of $1,227 annually. Concluded the ad: "The simplicity and durability of the Coulthard Steam Truck place it in the lead for the hard usage and severe service to which power trucks are subject." The $4,000 price tag, however, was high. Originally built by the American Coulthard Company, Boston, Mass., and Minneapolis, Minn., this vehicle was later manufactured by the Vaughn Machine Company, Peabody, Mass. Production span: 1905 to 1906. •

Covert

THE 1901 Standard Steam Carriage, Stanhope Model here shown was one of many automotive lines offered by a firm that handled everything from steam gauges to complete vehicles. The two-cylinder, vertical engine 2½x3½ in. with ball bearing crankshaft, produced five to seven hp. a 16 in. tubular boiler with an independent water pump generated 300 psi of working steam, and the water and fuel tanks were to order. Featuring chain drive and tiller steering, this buggy cost $800 complete; or the components could be bought separately. The complete chassis (without tires) for instance, sold for $125, the burner for $22, the engine for $130, the body (unfinished) $50, steam and air gauges and safety valves were $4 each, tires from $14 apiece, and the boiler cost $100. "The style of carriage illustrated is now considered 90 per cent standard of the steam carriages in use," stated the catalog. "Our purpose is not only to supply steam carriages but all principal parts required for the construction of carriages of this description." The firm also offered a "special lightweight Runabout equipped with a three hp air-cooled gasolene engine, and a two-speed transmission with reverse." This machine weighed 350 pounds, had a speed of eight to 12 mph and cost $500. Discounts of 10 to 25 per cent were offered the trade, "varying on different articles. Inquiries promptly and cheerfully answered." Despite all this activity, B. V. Covert & Company, of Lockport, N. Y., lasted only from 1901 to 1904.

The Eastman Metallic Stanhope body (above, right), "suitable for leading makes of Steam Automobiles," was one of numerous components offered in 1901 by the B. V. Covert Company. Price (unfinished) but with seat and dash was $63.50. Side panels could be obtained with wicker design at extra cost. Upholstery and paint also were additional. •

Crouch

IN DESIGN if not in appearance, the 1899 Crouch Steam Carriage reflected the ideals of an engineer truly interested in performance. The two-cylinder engine, 3x6 in., was a 90° V-type with poppet valves in the cylinder heads and an output of up to eight hp. Four sets of double pitch coils and a super-heating coil made up the boiler which was jacketed with asbestos and tested to 1,000 psi. Super-heated steam with 250-275 psi working pressure entered the engine at 650° F., obviating all moisture and condensation. The water tank held 16 gallons and the fuel tank 12 gallons of gas or kerosene. This light-weight scaled only 650 pounds and at an economical setting consumed less than 20 pounds of water (2½ gallons) per hour. On January 24, 1899, designer and builder W. Lee Crouch of New Brighton, Pa., drove 25 miles in deep mud with a 200-pound passenger and climbed "the worst hill in the county." He had no trouble keeping up with electric vehicles and "ran away from them" on the steepest hills. A week later, in company with a gentleman from Wheeling, West Va., Mr. Crouch drove from Rochester to Beaver Falls, Pa., over frozen, hilly, muddy roads covering 4½ miles in 15 minutes. No price was given for this versatile steam buggy, but the firm did business from 1897 to 1900 when it was absorbed by the Stanton Manufacturing Co. •

Curran

THIS EXPERIMENTAL 1928 Curran Steam Commercial Vehicle chassis was one more belated attempt to regain a foothold for steam power on the highway, but like so many others it came to a premature ending. Yet it featured many ideas that were the outcome of vastly improved technology in metals, thermodynamics and precision engineering. Motion was derived from a three-cylinder, horizontal, reciprocating steam engine of uniflow principle, with an improved valve action which regulated the entry of steam from five per cent to the full length of the stroke, according to power desired. Maximum output was 185 hp. The boiler, of a new design combining both water and fire tubes in an aluminum casing, provided working steam at 600 psi—a pretty high pressure. The Curran test steam bus, carrying an 11-ton load, was driven up various grades on the outskirts of New York City and averaged better than eight miles per gallon of kerosene. The burner worked equally well on any grade of fuel oil or gasoline, the vehicle developing one hp for every 22 pounds of steam consumed. High torque, a good power-weight ratio, smooth, flexible running and ease of operation were demonstrable features of this steamer designed by Frank J. Curran and Charles R. Nebelmesser. The press was cautious: "whether or not this portends a new development or revival, or whether it is in the end only a particularly good demonstration of an individual machine, time and future experiment alone will tell. . ." But it also came up with the old question: "Does it not . . . seem a curious fact that the steam automobile never attained wide production. . . ?"

An interesting and practical feature of the Curran Steam Bus was that the engine went dead as soon as the operator released the foot-pedal throttle. By acting as a brake, it took much of the strain and wear away from the wheel brakes —and this, with the bus constantly stopping and starting, would have meant quite a saving in operating costs. No price was quoted since the Curran never reached the production line, but that it failed to do so was due more than anything else to the fact that the inventors couldn't raise the many millions required to enter the competitive field with any chance of success.

The 1928 Curran Steam Bus chassis (see below) was thoroughly practical. The Duplex boiler was located under the hood, while the engine took the place of the conventional clutch and transmission. A short propellor shaft conveyed power to the rear axle, and also drove the air pump and electric generator through gears. Water tanks fitted snugly either side of the shaft and the main fuel tank was at the back. Steam condensation took place in a front-mounted "radiator." •

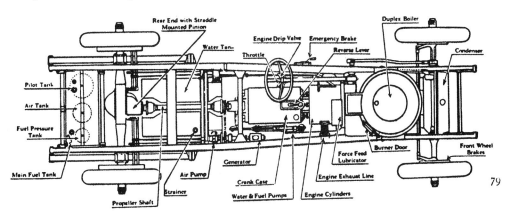

Dawson

THIS WAS THE DAWSON Steam Auto-Mobile of 1901, manufactured by a firm which did "a general machine business in addition to manufacturing autos." The two-cylinder engine (located under the seat) was a 2¾x4 in. job made from a brass casting. Rocker valves were a feature, together with "a set of eccentrics for reversing." The seamless sheet steel boiler contained 480 copper tubes and was tested to 1,000 psi, cold water. Working steam reached the engine at 220 psi. Water and gas capacity were 25 and eight gallons in tanks located within the body, and the weight was 1,100 pounds. On "fair roads," the Dawson would keep up a steady 25 to 30 mph. A brass burner of "new design" was employed, which produced a "blue flame." Three persons of ordinary size could ride comfortably abreast on the seat and steering was by tiller. External water level gauge may be seen below carriage lamp. Price of this machine was available "on request." Built by the Dawson Mfg. Co., Basic, Va., in a "large plant located on a five-acre tract," the Dawson Auto-Mobile disappeared in 1902 after a two-year life. •

Delling

THE 1923 Delling Steam Car, above, was another late comer seemingly foredoomed to failure; but by sheer excellence of design, coupled with great tenacity and adequate working capital, it remained on the market for 12 years. It had a two-cylinder, vertical, double-acting engine which conveyed power to the rear axle via a drive shaft. Boiler was a vertical water-tube type which (once the pilot burner was in operation) could raise steam at 600 psi in about 30 seconds. The burner used gasoline, kerosene or a mixture of these two in any proportion, at a rate of 16 to 18 mpg. Speed was from one to 60 mph. Drive was in high all the time, "as it has no transmission or clutch." This steamer was the brainchild of E. H. Delling,

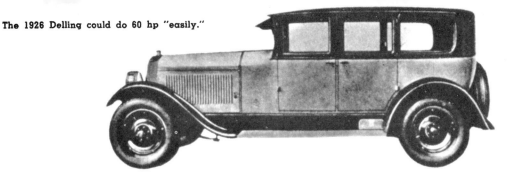

The 1926 Delling could do 60 hp "easily."

an outstanding engineer who produced it only after six years of "intensive study." Delling, who had designed the famous Mercer four-cylinder gas car, and was responsible for improving the Stanley Steamer, obviously knew what the score was. He felt confident that after 50,000 miles his car would run "as silently and smoothly as it did when it left the factory." At first one model only was offered—a Touring Car—which sold for $2,500; but the Delling Motors Co., of Philadelphia, Pa., founded in 1923, was destined to stage one of the two most effective revivals of steam transportation in the Twenties.

The 1926 Delling Steam Car, above, differed from its predecessors more in the matter of refinements than of fundamental design. It still had a two-cylinder, vertical, reversible engine (3¾x4½ in.) and the drive shaft carried power to the rear axle through a two-to-one reduction gear without transmission or clutch. The vertical water-tube boiler produced super-heated steam at a working pressure of 700 psi, and the burner was supplied from two fuel tanks (gas or kerosene) with a 32 gallon capacity. Weight of the Sedan was about 3,500 pounds for an outstanding performance. "Acceleration," it was claimed, "measured with a stop-watch, is approximately double that of gasoline cars. At 30 to 40 mph, the most noticeable sound is the singing of the tires on the road. The car runs so smoothly and silently that 40 mph

seems like 20." Maximum speed was unspecified, but 60 mph could be reached "easily." A contemporary automotive journal, reviewing the Delling, said: "Some folks like a steam car. Here is a new and improved design. Even after admitting that the majority of people will probably always prefer gasoline cars, the fact remains that the steam car has never had a fair chance. . ." The Delling was said to "glide away so silently it gives the impression that here is a car with no engine at all, which runs miraculously on its reputation—to paraphrase an old joke." Buyers now had the choice of a Phaeton at $2,895, or a Sedan for $3,200, both five-passenger jobs. Enough folks seemingly must have liked a steam car, for the Delling survived right on until 1934.

As seen from the 1926 chassis shown below, designer E. H. Delling stayed with a layout which embodied a compact vertical engine and boiler both located under the hood, and "conventional" shaft drive to the rear axle. Frame had deep side members for rigidity. Side filler cap supplied water tank.

Fuel and water pumps were tandem driven through a gear train from rear end of crankshaft on 1926 Delling Steam Engine, below. Note also external contracting transmission brake, a feature still common to many modern automobiles. Compactness and neatness were evident features of this engine design. •

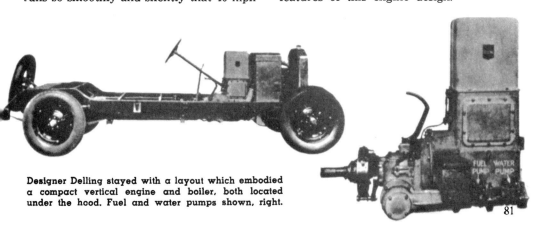

Designer Delling stayed with a layout which embodied a compact vertical engine and boiler, both located under the hood. Fuel and water pumps shown, right.

Detroit

SIMILAR in appearance to the average gasoline car then seen
on the roads, the 1922 Detroit Steamer (known also as the
Trask-Detroit) was a sturdy, reliable and moderately priced automobile. Its two-cylinder, slide-valve, double-acting engine of 10 hp
was of Uniflow type with Stephenson link valve gear and a bore and
stroke of 3¼x4¼ in. Claimed to produce "the equivalent in output
of a 45 to 50 hp gas car," it was geared direct to the rear axle. The
front-mounted fireproof water-tube boiler, made up of 628 flues,
built 500 psi of working steam pressure. Its burner could be fired on
low grade gasoline, kerosene or distillates with equal effect at a rate
of 15 to 20 mpg. A system of oil separation which clarified the exhaust
steam before it was condensed back into the water tank, greatly
increased the life and efficiency of the boiler. Weight was 2,000 pounds
with a cruising speed of 50 mph at 1,000 rpm, and the engine had only
40 moving parts. From 600 to 800 miles could be covered from one
filling of the water tank, and 2,000 miles on a gallon of lubricating
oil. Of handy size with a 110-in. wheelbase, the Detroit featured
electric lighting of the burner from a dash switch and an engine steam
throttle on the steering post. "Various manufacturing refinements"
were claimed by O. C. Trask who supervised the design. Mr. Trask
was a former partner of the Trask-Kennedy Company, Detroit, agent
for the Steamer and became president and treasurer of the new company, known as the Detroit Steam Motors Corp., Detroit, Michigan.
Formed in December 1921, this firm was assured of "ample financing"
by Boston bankers and did not place its stock on the market. In effect
it was the former Doble-Detroit Steam Motors Corp., reconstituted
after Abner Doble broke away to start a separate enterprise in California. Production got under way late in 1922 with a promise of five
body styles, but the Touring Car here seen, priced at $1,585, was the
only model to appear. Manufacture began at the Schlieder Manufacturing Company's plant (makers of valves), but by the end of the
year the project fizzled out. Competition in "the capital of motordom"
proved too tough. •

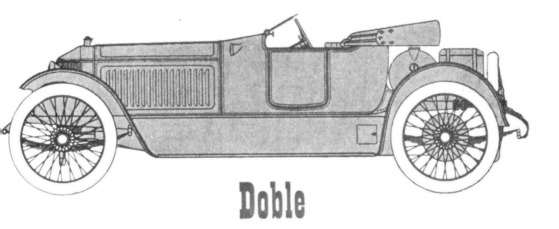

Doble

BY 1914 things looked pretty dim for the steam car. The White was already four years defunct, the Stanley Brothers remaining the only commercial champions of steam on the U. S. market. But that year, a brilliant engineer named Abner Doble threw down the gauntlet to the all-conquering gasoline automobile and began production of a completely new Steam Roadster. That the newcomer really had the goods was at once evident. The Doble steam engine was a two-cylinder, single-expansion horizontal power unit with locomotive-type slide valves, actuated by Joy valve gear. Of 4x6 in. bore and stroke, it produced 25 hp and drove the rear axle direct. Steam was built in a Stanley-type fire tube boiler located under the hood and made up of 1,001 steel tubes that offered 150 sq. ft. of heating surface. Superheated steam was quickly produced at a working pressure of 750 psi from water stored in a 25 gallon tank—enough for 1,000 miles. Kerosene fuel, carried in a 10 gallon tank, was consumed at the rate of 10 mpg.

Scaling around 2,800 pounds, the Doble Roadster had a sizzling performance: 0-60 mph in 15 secs., 75 mph easily. Its long (132 in.) wheelbase allowed ample room for a Phaeton body at the purchaser's choice. Said the contemporary press, with interest: "This new make of steam car may mark the recrudescence of an old type . . ." Abner Doble said nothing. He formed the Abner Doble Motor Vehicle Company, of Waltham, Mass., and incorporated it October 30, 1914, with a capital of $500,000. Then he just went ahead and built cars. During the early days, things were not too easy, due to the customary deep-rooted and unimaginative prejudice. In 1916 it was announced that the Abner Doble Steam

This 1913 Doble test car was driven for two years before being put into production.

Automobile would be marketed by a new enterprise—the General Engineering Company, incorporated with a capital of $200,000, and that the new president would be C. L. Lewis, former head of the Consolidated Car Company. But those who thought the Doble was all washed up had a big surprise coming.

The 1913 Doble test car (top of page 83) wire wheels and all, driven for two years over many thousands of miles before it finally went into production as the 1914 Roadster. The engine was geared direct to the rear axle—one to one.

The improved 1917 Double Steamer (bottom, page 83) was driven by a single-expansion, double-acting horizontal engine, 5x4 in., with modified Joy valve gear and

only 11 moving parts. Power unit put out 75 hp, the water-tube boiler (under the hood) building 600 psi of working steam from cold in two minutes. An improved kerosene burner was ignited by an electric spark, doing away with the old-fashioned pilot light which (on account of fire risks) often caused hard feelings between steam car enthusiasts and garage owners. With a 128-in. wheelbase, weight of this vehicle was 3,500 pounds. Price was not mentioned, and with confident pride Doble simply described his product as "The Ultimate Car."

A sectioned view of the 1917 Doble steam engine and "transmission" is shown at the top of the opposite page. It had a double-acting piston, ball-bearing connecting rod, spur gear drive from crankshaft to differ-

This improved 1917 Doble was described as "The Ultimate Car."

This is a sectioned view of the 1917 Doble steam engine and "transmission." Was precision engineered.

ential, and gear-driven pump inside rear tank. Precision engineering was evident throughout.

Superb in every respect was the 1923 Doble Steam Phaeton (below) with a custom body by Walter M. Murphy of Pasadena, California. Powered by a four-cylinder, cross-compound, double-acting engine, it derived steam from a water tube boiler that could raise 750 psi in less than a minute. Kerosene, gasoline or distillates were equally suitable for fuel and performance was an eye-opener. This steamer would do 80 mph any time, easily. Said the makers: "The De Luxe Doble is guaranteed for 100,000 luxurious, silent and trouble-free miles. Bodies are the last word in coach equipment and in some respects

partake of the luxurious appearance of the Rolls-Royce." The De Luxe Sport Phaeton here seen had its world premiere at the 1923 San Francisco Auto Show where it created a sensation. The body, hood and Disteel wheels were painted Ditzler pale auto yellow, with the rest of the car black. The radiator shell was nickel plated and 12-in. Rolls-Royce type drum-shaped headlamps were featured. In keeping was the $8,000 price tag. By March 1924, however, the firm of F. G. Cox, Inc., which had been conducting an intensive sales campaign for the Doble Steam Motors Corp., San Francisco, Calif., abandoned its efforts when Attorney General Sherman began an investigation with the Better Business Bureau. Seems that the Cox con-

Superb in every respect was the 1923 Doble Steam Phaeton. Custom body was designed by W. M. Murphy.

By 1925 Doble Steam Motors had obviously solved its problems with this De Luxe Phaeton.

cern had sold its allotment of Doble stock, but up to February 1, 1924, only eight Doble cars had been produced.

By 1925 Doble Steam Motors had obviously solved its problems, for this handsome De Luxe Steam Phaeton (above) was in full production and finding enough customers. A four-cylinder, horizontal, double-acting compound engine, 2⅝ and 4½x5 in., equipped with piston valves, supplied motive power. The water tube steam generator, made up of 36 sections, produced between 600 and 750 psi working pressure in 30 to 45 seconds merely by turning a key. The water tank held 17 gallons and the fuel tank (kerosene or gasoline) 26 gallons. Weight was around 3,600 pounds which the power unit could propel at a continuous 75 mph with ease. The chassis frame, of heated and treated chrome nickel steel, had seven tubular cross members for stiffness, nothing being omitted which could contribute to luxury, efficiency and smooth riding. Three models were offered, including a Limousine and a Phaeton, all in the luxury class.

Gadget-laden appearance of 1925 Doble chassis (opposite page) belied the basic simplicity of design. A horizontal engine, cast in two pairs of cylinders, was unit-built with rear axle which it drove direct. Fuel tank was in the usual place, with the water tank under the front compartment. Battery was carried on right side of frame and vertical boiler fitted snugly under the hood. A large fan with 24 in. blades, turning 3,200 rpm at 60 mph, was used to cool steam in the condenser-radiator which returned its contents to the water tank. Road springs were 58 in. long in the rear and 44 in. in front.

Magnificent was a word that aptly described the 1926 Convertible Doble (opposite page, bottom). It had a four-cylinder, double-acting, compound, horizontal engine with two high-pressure cylinders, 2⅝x5 in., and two low-pressure 4½x5 in. Displacement was 3,490 cc, the output being 119.6 hp at 937 rpm. A flash type vertical boiler provided superheated steam at 710 psi working pressure was supplied with water from a 30 gallon tank—enough for 750 miles. Gasoline capacity was 26 gallons and vehicle weight 4,256 pounds. This Doble could raise full steam in less than a minute and would do 60 mph at only 900 rpm. Maximum speed was better than 95 mph. Gas consumption: eight mpg in town and 11 mpg on the open road. The engine was geared direct to the rear axle and oil consumption was stated to be quite low—up to 4,000 mpg. Said a steam enthusiast: "What a boon it would be to city life, and how pleasant our cities would be, if all mechanically operated road transport could be driven by some prime mover that made no noise in starting, had no roaring engine, had no gearbox and could move off with scarcely a sound. And yet that is what can be done with that much misunderstood (by the public) and old-established prime mover, the steam engine. That the steam car has been so neglected since the days when it was common—from 1900 to 1910—is due largely to the fact that only in comparatively recent years has boiler technique advanced to a position which enables a satisfactory and reliable boiler to be produced." Of the Doble, it was claimed: "The low engine speed of this steam car gives a freedom from wear and an ease of maintenance which are great advantages." Price range of the Doble Steam Motors Corporation started around $3,000, f.o.b. San Francisco but the 14-year life span of this amazing steamer was almost at an end. Little more than a year of it remained. •

Gadget-laden appearance of the 1925 Doble chassis, above, belied its basic simplicity. Magnificent was the word for the 1926 Convertible Doble, below, which could raise a full head of steam in less than a minute.

Doble-Detroit

THIS 1918 Doble-Detroit seven-passenger Steam Touring Car was the product of a new enterprise formed in Detroit to manufacture Doble automobiles, in succession to the General Engineering Company. A two-cylinder, uniflow, double-acting, single-expansion, slide-valve engine of horizontal type (4x5-in.) supplied the urge, producing some 75 hp. The boiler was a Doble-Detroit vertical water tube unit with 123 sq. ft. of heating surface. Water and kerosene tanks each held 25 gallons, and the resultant performance was something to talk about. This steamer could "creep along at less than one mph and accelerate instantly and smoothly to express train speed." The press, careful as usual, expressed itself thus: "There is nothing freakish or unusual in the appearance of the Doble Detroit Steam Car. It conforms to the most advanced standards of automobile design and is a car of beauty, distinction and character. There are only 22 moving parts in the entire car." As indicated by the lavish details, fine workmanship and resultant high price of $3,750, Doble's brainchild had now blossomed out into a luxury job. But within three years a rift occurred in the Doble Detroit Steam Motors Corporation, Detroit, Michigan.

Once again that genius, Abner Doble, was on the move—this time to California where he formed an entirely new company on his own. In February 1922 came an announcement that the Doble Steam Car was to be manufactured by Doble Steam Motors, San Francisco, with production scheduled to start August 1. Production for

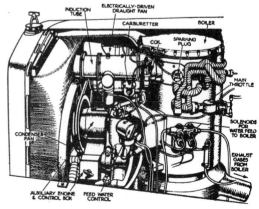

the rest of that year was not expected to exceed 30 cars, but a 300 car output was planned for 1923. Abner Doble, long a figure in the steam car field, was named president; W. A. Doble, Jr., general manager. The new car was to be named the Doble-Simplex and would probably cost about $2,000.

A sectional view of the Steam Generator (opposite page, bottom left) shows flow of combustion gases marked by large arrows; small arrows indicate flow of water which entered lower headers of the Economizer Section at right. Steam then left the upper headers of the Evaporating Section located above combustion chamber. Superheated steam reached engine at 600 psi. and a temperature of about 485° F.

The flash boiler of the 1918 Doble Detroit Steamer (opposite page, bottom right) was a marvel of ingenuity. Solenoid switches controlled the water feed and the burner was ignited by a spark plug at the turn of a key. An electrically driven fan supplied the required amount of air. Steam at 600 psi could be raised in two minutes. •

Eclipse

SHORT LIVED was the 1902 Eclipse Steam Vehicle, featured as a Runabout. It had a three-cylinder engine with piston valves and an output of eight hp. Crankshaft and all moving parts were "perfectly counterbalanced." A water tube boiler, 20 in. in diameter, built steam at 180 psi, the burner featuring a pilot light. The oversize water tank held 60 gallons against 25 gallons of gasoline. This Runabout tipped the scales at 1,000 pounds and sold for exactly a dollar per pound. The engine was geared by bevel pinion and gear to a "compensating gear" on the rear axle, and all machinery was hung on an angle iron frame. "Graceful design, unusual roominess and striking constructional features," were claimed. The most interesting achievement of the Eclipse, however, took place on January 21, 1901, when the firm signed a contract with Boston post office officials to deliver three motor carriages to be placed in commission March 1. "Postmaster Hanson of Back Bay Station," said the announcement, "feels confident these three wagons will take the place of seven horse-drawn wagons and will reduce mail collection time by 20 minutes." Founded in 1900, the Eclipse Automobile Company, Boston, Mass., survived until 1903. •

Elite

THIS ORNATE 1901 Steam Victoria with scrollwork on the dash and tiller side steering, fared no better than most other steam buggies of the day. Its two-cylinder, slide-valve engine was claimed to have 22 less parts and to be "heavier and stronger than any other steam engine used in an automobile." For the sake of simplicity, link-motion was dispensed with. The boiler, made up of 420 copper tubes, featured a Kelly burner and pilot light and produced steam at 160 psi working pressure. Fuel (gasoline) capacity was 10 gallons; weight 1,350 pounds. An ingenious feature of the Elite was a dual purpose auxiliary steam-driven pump which either maintained air pressure in the gas tank or pumped water into the constant level boiler in case of emergency. The seat afforded "sufficient space for three persons" and the body and running gear were finished in black with carmine stripes. Dash, tail lamps, hubs and steering handle were of highly polished brass with gold finish; upholstery was maroon. Besides this steamer, D. B. Smith & Co., Utica, New York, also built a Saratoga Tourist Gasoline Car of similar appearance. Said maker, playing it safe: "This automobile, as is signified by the name, is built and designed only for the finest trade and cannot fail to please the most fastidious." And of the Steam Victoria: "It will attract attention and command admiration wherever seen. It is a perfect automobile and not a horseless carriage." The Elite lasted one year. •

Empire

INTRODUCED in 1904, the Empire Steam Touring Car (bottom, opposite page) had a two-cylinder, horizontal, 15 hp engine with Stephenson link valve gear. Boiler was of the semi-flash water tube type, supplied from a 40 gallon water tank giving a 40 mile range. Enough gasoline for 125 miles (15 gallons) was carried, and the weight of this Tonneau job was 1,970 pounds. Endeavoring to gain public's con-

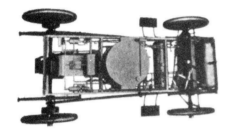

fidence, makers declared: "The car now offered for the season of 1904 is not an untried model. It is the result of four years' experimentation and investigation by the inventor, William H. Terwilliger, who has made a life study of steam engineering." Added was this exclusive note: "The makers do not anticipate a large output this year. They will construct only 40 cars, each under the supervision of the inventor." Tonneau model was the only one offered, but William H. Terwilliger & Company, of Amsterdam, N. Y., failed to prosper. A year later the firm was out of business. Chassis of 1904 Empire Steam Touring Car, left, featured a front-mounted water tank; fuel tank under the driving seat, boiler amidships and engine at the back, unit-constructed with the rear axle to which it was geared direct. Pumps were engine driven. Weight distribution was reasonably good. •

Foster

WHAT THE 1904 Foster Steam Wagon lacked in beauty of line, it certainly made up in performance and reliability. Yet the design was nothing unusual. A two-cylinder, five hp vertical engine derived steam from a 16-in. fire-tube boiler tested to 1,000 psi steam pressure which built 180 psi of working pressure. With 35 gallons of water and enough gas for 125 miles, weight was 1,285 pounds. As to performance, this little steamer (claimed able to climb a 10 per cent grade at 30 mph) scooped enough trophies and gold medals to convince anyone. These included the New York to Buffalo Endurance Run, September 13, 1901; and the New York-Boston Reliability Run, October 1902, in which it defeated cars costing up to $7,000 among 97 entries and finished with a perfect score. In 1903, when the Artzberger Automobile Company took over the Foster Steam Wagon concern in Allegheny, Pa., these successes continued. A Foster won the Auto Club of Pittsburgh's Highland Park Hillclimb, June 20, 1903, beating all steam cars and every gasoline car but one It also won the Highland Park Straight-

away Race, June 11, defeating all comers over the mile and uphill. The new owners were responsible for various improvements such as a double-acting brake; a longer (75-in.) wheelbase and a lower center of gravity; and a new type of slot burner. "It leads them all!" they claimed. "Here is a machine strong, durable, economical, handsome and well equipped." The 1904 Steam Touring Car shown cost $650 and was lowest-priced in a three model range with a high of $1,000. But the test of time was too great. First built in 1900, the Foster went out of production in 1905. •

Gearless

ONE OF FOUR new makes to appear in 1921 when the steam car staged a come-back, this Gearless Runabout held the promise of originality. Power was supplied by two separate two-cylinder, double-acting, slide valve engines with Walchaert link motion, each driving one rear wheel by direct crank action. The water tube boiler, made up of Nichols Steel Alloy tubes, offered 114 sq. ft. of heating surface and produced working steam at 210 psi. The water tank held 25 gallons and the weight was 2,600 pounds. "Up to 70 mph" was claimed by manufacturer who described the Gearless design thus: "By using two steam engines, each one operating one rear wheel, this new steam car does away with the necessity of a differential for the rear axle. Both engines are controlled by a single throttle and differential action is secured without the use of gears. These are Facts—not Hopes nor Dreams. The Gearless is a Common Sense car with no tender or delicate parts." A two-model range included the Roadster at $2,650 and the Touring Car for $100 less. Exhibited at the Hotel Commodore, N. Y., June 7-14, 1922, the Gearless brought favorable comment, but less than a year later—in May 1923—the storm broke. Four officers of the Gearless Motor Corp., Pittsburgh, Pa., were indicted by a Federal Grand Jury charged with using the mails to defraud and with conspiracy. They were accused of selling $1,360,000 worth of company stock under false representation. This was the swan song of the Gearless firm but it left open a puzzling aspect of the public's psychology. Time and again, brokerage firms had little trouble in selling steam car

stock issues to individuals even though motorists had long since clearly expressed their preference for gasoline cars. How did investors expect to get a return on their money?

The Steam Touring Car (top photo) followed "standard practice in chassis and body design. It sold for $2,550. Identical chassis was used for the Runabout except for wire wheels.

The duplex horizontal steam unit, above, had four cylinders, 3x6 in. Each engine functioned independently, driving a rear wheel direct. Throttle compensation took the place of a differential on curves. Smoothly encased water-tube boiler, right, was a snug fit under the hood. As usual, exhaust steam was condensed in radiator. •

Geneva

STYLED "The most luxuriant two-passenger Steam Road Car made," this 1903 Geneva Style "C" Runabout had some claim to originality. A two-cylinder, six hp marine type engine was used, 2½x3½ in., and the water-tube boiler held 17 ft. of coiled tubing. Tested to 600 psi, it produced 160 psi of working pressure. Water was derived from a 40-gallon tank—sufficient for 35 to 50 miles on country roads; gasoline (8 to 15 gallons) gave a cruising range of 100 to 150 miles. This Style "C" Runabout tipped 950 pounds, was claimed "able to climb any hill," and would do up to 50 mph. Of its patented boiler and burner, makers had this to say: "Beware of patent infringement as we shall protect our patents against all makers or users of boilers which infringe upon ours. The Geneva Steam Car is equipped with the best and most economical burner on the market and also with a pilot light. It is equalled by few and surpassed by none." Offered were four models "upholstered in high-grade leather," with a price range of $900 for the Runabout here shown, to $1,200 for the Model "C" Surrey. The Geneva Automobile and Manufacturing Company, Geneva, Ohio, started business in 1901 but was through by 1904. •

Grout

THE GROUT BROTHERS Automobile Company, Orange, Mass., builders of this 1901 Queen Steam Stanhope, were among the earliest comers in the steam car industry. Of typical horseless buggy appearance, this steamer featured a two-cylinder, four hp double-acting engine with chain drive to the rear axle. Steam was derived from a water-tube boiler tested to 600 psi which produced 180 psi of working steam and had a safety valve set at 260 psi. A copper water tank held 21 gallons and 8½ gallons of "gasolene" fuel were carried. Weight, complete, was 1,000 pounds. "We will go as fast as any steam vehicle," claimed maker, "and we will climb any hill that ever was climbed." The early Grout achieved several distinctions,

including a silver medal at the Philadelphia Auto and Cycle Show for being the best constructed steam vehicle. "Steam is our power," said an ad, "the only reliable power known for autos. We make every part in our own factory, which was the first built in the U. S. especially for manufacturing autos. The Grout has no speed-changing gear; change of speed is accomplished by engine throttle, the same as a locomotive. The vehicle may be left standing for hours with the main burner out, and you can relight the burner without a match from the seat and start at once." Humorously uncompromising was this statement: "We experimented with gasoline or hydro-carbon and built many of these wagons, but could not see in what

Sentry Box appearance of the 1901 Grout "New Home" Steam Coupe was thought handsome by many.

respect they could be compared favorably to steam." The 1901 range offered five models from $750 to $900 for the Queen Stanhope, but the firm (founded in 1897) chewed up its words when it started making gasoline autos in 1904, and swallowed them the following year when steam car production was dropped altogether.

Sentry Box appearance of the 1901 Grout "New Home" Steam Coupe (above) was thought handsome by many. Specifications were similar to other models, except that the gas tank held 6½ gallons and the weight was 1,500 pounds. Priced at a dollar per pound, this Coupe was claimed to have "good style for a physician."

A "progressive" ad for the Grout Steam Wagon featured a skeleton (top picture, page 97) with the legend: "The Passing of the Horse. These animals were used until about the year 1901."

Seen in 1901 was the "West Side Assembly Room" (bottom photo, page 97) of the Grout factory in Orange, Mass.

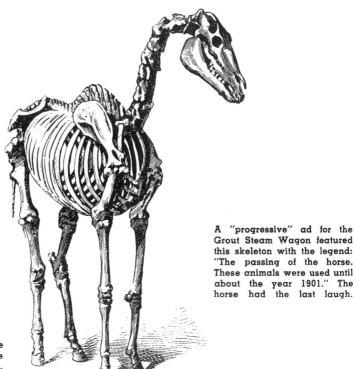

A "progressive" ad for the Grout Steam Wagon featured this skeleton with the legend: "The passing of the horse. These animals were used until about the year 1901." The horse had the last laugh.

This was the busy "West Side Assembly Room" in 1901 in the Grout factory, Orange, Mass.

Last of the Grout Steamers, this 1905 Touring Car (above), blunt snouted, half auto, half locomotive, was certainly no thing of beauty. It had a two-cylinder, 12 hp, slide-valve engine enclosed in an aluminum case, and "after careful consideration of the water tube and flash generator," the boiler featured a "superheater and steam dryer." From cold, a full head could be raised in five minutes. With 45 gallons of water and 15 of gasoline, this steamer could lug its 1,750 pounds weight at 18 to 25 mph and climb a 25 to 30 per cent grade with a full load. Already in the gasoline auto field since the previous year, the firm played both ends against the middle with remarkable nerve. In an ad headed "Gasoline versus Steam" it brazenly stated: "There is not a single gasoline expert living who can be certain when he turns the crank of a gasoline motor that it will even start—to say nothing of what power it will develop

or how long it will run, even after it has started. That is far beyond him. A gasoline engine at its best is a most complicated affair." Produced in one model only, the 1905 Grout steamer sold for $1,500 and was finished in "beautiful carmine or Merrimac green." It was claimed "not built for speed but for reliability." Switching to a four-cylinder gasoline car in 1904 prolonged the life of the Grout Automobile Company until 1912, but it had a turbulent existence and during that time was twice in the hands of the receiver.

Features of 1905 Grout steamer chassis (below) were a front-mounted vertical boiler, a horizontal engine located amidships (which drove the rear axle by chains through a countershaft), gas tank under the driving seat and a huge flat water tank under the rear compartment. Chassis layout showed no more beauty or imagination than did the body. •

1 Engine in aluminum case	7 Countershaft	13 Compensating gear	18 Cast burner, one piece
2 Boiler	8 Klinger gauge with shut-off	14 Force feed oiler	19 Forced draft
3 Water tank, 45 gallons	9 Auxiliary throttle	15 Power air pump	20 Hand water pump
4 Gasoline tank, 15 gallons	10 Reverse lever	16 Air pump control	21 Ejector
5 Air tank	11 Balanced throttle	17 Automatic fire regulator	22 Power water pump
6 Steering check	12 Muffler		

STEAM CAR GEOGRAPHY

THE 83 makes of manufactured steamers reviewed in this book, covering a period of over 40 years, originated in 59 different cities located in 18 states and the District of Columbia. Most prolific in steam car production was Massachusetts with 13 cities. New York State was next with 12 cities and Pennsylvania third with six.

Breakdown was as follows:

CALIFORNIA . . . . San Francisco
CONNECTICUT . . . Bridgeport, New Haven
DIST. COLUMBIA . . Washington
ILLINOIS . . . . . . Elgin, Lanark, Sterling
INDIANA . . . . . . Richmond
KANSAS . . . . . . Parsons
MAINE . . . . Brunswick, Lewiston
MARYLAND . . . . Luke
MASSACHUSETTS . . Boston, Chicopee Falls, Danvers, Dorchester, Everett, Marlborough, Newtonville, Orange, Salem, Springfield, Waltham, Westfield, Worcester
MICHIGAN . . . . . Detroit, Hudson, Jackson
MISSOURI . . . . . St. Louis
NEW HAMPSHIRE . . Keene, Manchester
NEW JERSEY . . . . Camden, Passaic, Trenton
NEW YORK . . . . . Amsterdam, Brooklyn, Buffalo, Cohoes, Lockport, Newburgh, New York, Poughkeepsie, Rochester, Syracuse, Tarrytown, Utica
OHIO . . . . Cleveland, Columbus, Garfield, Geneva
PENNSYLVANIA . . Allegheny, Carlisle, New Brighton, Philadelphia, Pittsburgh, Reading
RHODE ISLAND . . . Pawtucket
VIRGINIA . . . . . . Basic
WISCONSIN . . . . Milwaukee

PRODUCTION SPAN OF MANUFACTURED STEAM VEHICLES

American	1922-1924	Foster	1900-1905	New England	1899-1900
American Waltham	1898-1899	Gearless	1921-1923	New York	1900-1901
Amoskeag	1867-1906	Geneva	1901-1904	Porter	1900-1901
Baker	1921-1928	Grout	1897-1905	Prescott	1901-1905
Boss	1903-1907	Halsey	1906-1907	Puritan	1901-1904
Binney & Burnham	1902-1903	Hoffman	1902-1904	Reading	1900-1903
Brecht	1902-1904	Hood	1900-1901	Richmond	1902-1903
Brooks	1924-1930	Howard	1900-1904	Rochester	1900-1901
Capitol	1902-1903	Hudson	1901-1902	Roper	1860-1894
Century	1899-1902	Jaxon	1903-1904	Ross	1905-1909
Clark	1895-1909	Jenkins	1901-1902	Scott-Newcomb	1921-1922
Cloughley	1902-1903	Johnson	1906-1907	Skene	1900-1901
Coats	1922-1923	Kensington	1900-1903	Stanley	1897-1925
Coldwell	1903-1905	Kidder	1900-1901	Steamobile	1900-1904
Conrad	1900-1903	Lane	1900-1909	Stearns	1900-1903
Cotta	1901-1903	Leach	1899-1900	Sterling	1901-1902
Coulthard	1905-1906	Locomobile	1899-1903	Sunset	1901-1904
Covert	1901-1904	MacDonald	1923-1924	Sweany	1895-1896
Crouch	1897-1900	Marlboro	1899-1902	Toledo	1901-1903
Curran	1928-1929	Maryland	1900-1901	Tractobile	1900-1902
Dawson	1901-1902	Meteor	1902-1903	Twombly	1904-1905
Delling	1923-1934	Milwaukee	1900-1902	Victor	1899-1904
Detroit	1921-1923	Mobile	1899-1903	Westfield	1902-1903
Doble	1914-1929	Moncrief	1901-1902	White	1901-1910
Eclipse	1900-1903	Morgan	1903-1904	Whitney	1898-1905
Elite	1900-1901	Morse	1904-1906	Whitney Automatic	1897-1898
Empire	1904-1905	National	1899-1900	Wood	1902-1903
		Neustadt-Perry	1902-1903	Wood-Loco	1901-1902

Halsey

THIS 1906 Type 3D Steam Truck was a determined attempt by the James T. Balsey Motor Truck Company, Philadelphia, Pennsylvania, to break into the commercial vehicle field with a steamer. Two engines, each of four cylinders, were coupled direct to the front wheels. Of single-acting type, each produced 30 hp at 1,000 rpm and had a very low piston speed of 500 feet per minute. The big water-tube boiler was fed from a tank that held 180 gallons—enough for 15 to 20 miles, supplying both engines. Fuel could be either 500 pounds of pea grade coal or the equivalent in kerosene oil, giving a range of 30 miles "or one day's run." This truck was claimed able to carry an eight-ton load at six mph for less than one cent per ton-mile of fuel. Eight tons could thus be carried 40 miles for a dollar, which was "cheaper than gasolene by 75 per cent." Other claims were that "Halsey motors have been used on stationary engines for a number of years. The steam ports are tight under any condition and the noiseless front-wheel drive does the work of horse-drawn vehicles with eight or 10 horses and infinitely more, without getting tired. The steel rims wear two years or longer." On test, a Halsey steam engine ran "10 to 15 hours a day for a number of years without requiring the least attention or repairs, except for the usual oil cups." The firm built trucks of "any capacity," but the price with Standard chassis was according to body. Despite the many desirable attributes of steam, this concern lasted only from 1906 to 1907.

Vertical section of 1906 Halsey steam engine (below) showed common crankpin of cylinders. This unit was used on the Eight Ton truck, the company having built 10 different steam engines, from 10 to 500 hp. •

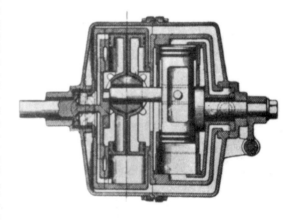

Hoffman

THE 1904 Hoffman Steam Car, above, was manufactured by a firm which also built gasoline autos while waiting to see which way the cat was going to jump. Power was derived from a two-cylinder, marine type engine of 6½ hp with 3x4 in. bore and stroke. A tubular boiler supplied superheated steam at 200 psi, but was tested to withstand a cold water pressure of 1,200 psi. Carried were 40 gallons of water and 14 of gasoline for a weight of 1,200 pounds. "As a hill climber," said maker, "no power equals steam. The Hoffman will climb any hill to which the wheels will stick. He added: "It will be the policy of this company to maintain the established reputation for the superior quality of the Hoffman brand of goods." Model shown cost $1,200, or $75 more with top. A year earlier, the Hoffman Automobile and Man-ufacturing Company of Cleveland, Ohio, had changed its name to the Royal Motor Car Company and in 1904 it began producing the Royal Tourist gasoline car. The shift came just in time, for the steamer was through that year. •

Hood

THE ELECTRONOMIC Safety Steam Vehicle was an imposing name for this spidery-looking 1901 Hood, but it did, for a change, embody some new ideas. Four single-acting cylinders supplied the power, each having a magnetic admission valve, while the exhaust ports were opened by the pistons. The intake valves were operated by three small electric batteries which provided enough current for over six months' use. Super-heated steam was built in a flash boiler with an operating pressure of 200 psi, made up from seven 20 ft. lengths of coiled steam pipe. The water tank held a 50-mile supply and the kerosene or gasoline fuel lasted 75 miles. Weight of this machine was 800 pounds; performance up to 30 mph on level roads. It was said to climb all ordinary grades. Among desirable features: "All valve cams, eccentric links and stuffing boxes are dispensed with. The running gear is simple and straight, with standard wheels, and permits the use of almost any kind of body." Model shown cost $1,000. It was built by the Simplex Motor Vehicle Company, Danvers, Mass., incorporated April 1900. By 1901 this firm was on its way out. •

Howard

ONE OF 19 new steamers which flooded the market in 1900, this 1901 Steam Runabout was neither better nor worse than the others and certainly looked no different. Its two-cylinder vertical engine, 2½x3½ in., used link reverse action; and the water-tube boiler supplied working steam at 175 psi from a 19 gallon water tank. Five gallons of gas were carried and the weight was 500 pounds. Final drive was by chain and the firm made no particular claims, except that it also built a Steam Truck. This buggy cost $750 and was on the market until 1904 when the Howard Auto Company, Trenton, N. J., called it quits. •

Hudson

LAUNCHED in 1901 with 13 other makes of steam buggies, the Hudson Steam Automobile featured a two-cylinder, vertical, reversible engine with both cylinders cast in "one piece." The tubular boiler featured a "low water alarm" and was replenished by an auxiliary hand pump. It built working steam at 160 psi, from a 21-gallon water tank. Six gallons of gas were carried; weight was 650 pounds and speed about 25 mph. It was equipped with chain drive, conventional carriage springs and tiller steering. Built by the Beau-Chamberlain Manufacturing Company, Hudson, Mich., this little steamer was no relation to the Hudson gasoline car. It lasted a little over a year. •

Jaxon

THIS 1903 JAXON Model "A" Open Steam Surrey (above) was the product of a firm organized in October that year which was simultaneously building gasoline cars. Its three-cylinder, vertical engine of six hp drove the rear axle by chain, and a 19-in. tubular boiler with "water alarm" supplied working steam at 160 psi. Carried were 35 gallons of water and 10 of gasoline. Tipping 1,500 pounds, this steamer featured "automatic lubrication" and at $975 was the costlier of two models with a low of $800. Folding front seat made room for four passengers and the finish generally was good. Built by the Jackson Automobile Company, Jackson, Michigan, it lasted only about a year, but the firm stayed in business manufacturing gasoline autos right on until 1922. •

Jenkins

THE 1901 JENKINS Observation Automobile (opposite page, bottom) was a progressive attempt at an early date to build a large and practical steam bus. The engine was a horizontal, four-cylinder, double compound job of 20 to 30 hp which supplied power through a differential shaft to ring gears clamped on the inside of the rear wheels. A modified marine-type water-tube boiler was used, and the water and kerosene tanks carried sufficient for 25 and 50 miles respectively. Claimed the builders: "This coach will travel in infinite graduations from the slowest speed up to 18 or 20 mph on smooth roads, and will climb any wagon road hill without the use of clutches or gear changes of any kind." This vehicle, stated to be the largest auto coach in America in its time, ran on 40 in. rear and 36 in. front wheels with 3½ in. solid rubber tires. Accommodation was provided for 22 passengers seated on rotary chairs in two compartments and the interior was lavishly appointed in hard woods and mirrors. External color scheme was dark green and black with striped gold leaf. The engine made "no puffing noise," and was "fully incased." The manufacturer agreed to furnish a new burner free of cost for every one that burned out. The Jenkins was built primarily for the Observation Auto Company, "to transport sight-seers about the national capital under guidance of an entertaining lecture." It was the product of the Jenkins Automobile Company, Washington, D. C., until 1902. •

Johnson

THE JOHNSON 1907 Tonneau Steam Car shown above was one of two new makes of steamers which appeared in 1906, only to disappear a year later without a ripple in the pool of oblivion. Featured was a four-cylinder, single-acting, 30 hp horizontal engine, 3¾x4 in. which drove the rear axle through a propeller shaft in "direct transmission." The Johnson nested tube boiler contained a single tube, 450 ft. long, coiled to fit the casing. Steam at 200 psi was generated by a kerosene burner and a 30 gallon water tank. With a 2,400-pound weight, 30 to 40 mph was possible and the machine would tackle "almost any grade." A handbrake on the rear hubs was controlled by "three hand wheels," the equipment including tools and extra pilots and retorts. Offered in one model priced at $1,500 by the Johnson Service Company, Milwaukee, Wisconsin, this steamer was a flop. •

Kensington

ANNOUNCED in 1900, this Kensington Steam Runabout was the product of "manufacturers of several styles of electric carriages who are building, also, a steam carriage on the usual lines as to form." It had a two-cylinder, four hp, double-acting, reversible link engine and an upright tubular boiler tested to 600 psi which produced 160 psi of normal working pressure. Some 25 to 30 miles could be covered with the water supply, while the gas tank offered a 50-mile range. Weighing 650 pounds, the Kensington featured a double-acting brake "in place of the usual single-acting brake." It also had a "starting device for getting up steam without use of a torch." Flexible speed from one to 35 mph and easy climbing of grades up to 36 per cent were claimed. The enclosed engine used splash lubrication. All these commodities were offered in one package for $750, but the Kensington Automobile Co., Buffalo, N. Y., decided to play it safe. It not only continued building electric cars, but in 1902 also announced a gasoline auto. Even this didn't help, and by 1904 the firm was out of business. •

Kidder

THIS 1901 Model No. 2 Kidder Steam Vehicle, "A Smart Steam Carriage of New Design," was the outcome of an ideal. Wellington P. Kidder, owner of Connecticut's Kidder Press, built two experimental steam wagons of his own design. The second one worked so satisfactorily that he succeeded in interesting other capitalists although he himself was "worth a fortune." The result was the formation of the Kidder Motor Vehicle Co., New Haven, Conn., in January 1900, with a capital of $5,000,000 and some $50,000 worth of machinery on order. The Kidder steam buggy used two separate cylinders 2½x3½ in., each of three hp, located on either side of the boiler. The horizontal engine cranked the rear axle by the "Kidder System of Direct Drive." A tubular boiler was used, made up of 326 copper tubes tested to 1,000 psi cold water pressure. This produced 200 psi working steam pressure and featured a condenser with 70 sq. ft. of cooling surface for water economy. The water tank held 30 gallons and the gasoline tank six gallons. Curb weight of the vehicle was 1,000 pounds. An interesting feature was the "universal joint connecting rods to the crankshaft which has a spur pinion directly engaging the spur differential driving gear." Model No. 2 at $1,000 was the lower priced of two types; the other being a commercial vehicle which cost $1,600. Started by "burning a few spoonfuls of alcohol in a heating pan," the Kidder did not fulfill its promise and the firm wound up operations in 1901. •

Lane

"STEAM IS THE MOST POWERFUL and obedient force known today," said the makers of this 1901 Model No. 1 Lane Steam Runabout (above), vindicating their choice of motive power. The engine was a two-cylinder, double-acting job, 3x4½ in., with ball bearings throughout. Working steam at 180 psi could be raised by the tubular boiler in "one minute." Enough water for 20 miles (25 gallons) was carried, and two gas tanks each held six gallons. Easily able to lug its 950 pound weight at 25 mph, the Lane Runabout held a First Class Certificate from the Auto Club of America for an endurance contest from New York to Rochester, September 9 to 13, 1901, for covering 390 miles at 12.25 mph. Following "points of superiority" were claimed: "The crankshaft is made from one solid billet of steel. Our peculiar burner of increased efficiency provides odorless combustion, durability and simplicity. We have undertaken to produce vehicles that will be *satisfactory* in customers' hands . . ." Able to run "a week or two without attention or oiling," Model No. 1 (with folding front seat) sold for $950 and was third lowest priced in a

six model range between $750 and $1,400. It was built by the Lane Motor Vehicle Company, Poughkeepsie, New York, who opened their doors in 1895 and closed them for good in 1909.

Looking as though the top were put on backward, this 1905 Lane Style 6 Touring Car (opposite page, top) had blossomed into a bigger, heavier, more powerful auto. The engine was a two-cylinder, compound, horizontal job of 15 hp, 3¼ and 5¼x3½ in. The patented 20 in. fire-tube boiler was claimed 43 per cent more efficient and offering greater reserve than the flash type. The water tank held 20 and the gas tank 17 gallons for a weight of 2,250 pounds. Of performance, makers claimed: "The Lane hill climbing ability is unexcelled and its speed possibilities are all that should be required for pleasure riding." Gas consumption figured at around 7 to 10 mpg. "The Lane Steam Car, Style No. 6 is the result of six years' experience in building steam vehicles" said the catalog. "The car is heavy enough for stability, large enough for comfort, hung on easy springs, luxuriously upholstered . . . There is no unpleasant vibration or noise from the motor, and because of the condenser no exhaust noise." Awarded highest percentage of points in the New York-Boston Endurance Run, the Lane covered 488.4 miles with a score of 99.8 per cent in competition with 55 gasoline, one electric and 19 steam cars. It also earned highest marks in the Auto Club of America's 100-Mile Long Island Contest, beating 50 gasoline and 16 steam cars. Costliest in a three-model range starting at $2,100, this steamer sold for $2,400 with a "full aluminum King of the Belgians" body, folding top and removable side curtains.

The Model 7 Steam Touring Car of 1907 (opposite page, left) showed detail improvements over its forerunners. Power of the two-cylinder, double-acting, cross-compound engine was boosted to 20 hp with same bore and stroke as formerly. The Lane "indestructible steam generator" was a semi-flash water-tube boiler, 20 in. in diameter which built 210 psi working pressure, supplied by a 20-gallon water tank and a 17-gallon gas tank. Weight was 2,300 pounds; speed from one to 40 mph. Despite short (97 in.) wheelbase, the French "Tulip Type" aluminum body seated five comfortably. Timken roller bearings were used throughout, except for the engine, and the front-mounted Lane condenser with vertical brass tubes helped steam economy. "All products of combustion pass beneath the car," claimed makers, "so

Shown on this page are the 1905 Lane Style 6 Touring Car, right; the 1907 Steam Touring Car, below; chassis of the 1905 Style 6, right center, and (bottom) the 1909 Model 17 seven-passenger Touring Car.

there is no heat or smell under the seats." Less costly of two types, Model 7 brought $2,500. A larger Model 7-5 with a 112 in. wheelbase, 30 hp engine, 50 mph speed and 2,700 pound weight cost $3,400.

Chassis of the 1905 Lane Style No. 6 steamer (right) featured a vertical boiler (with fusible plug) and water tank under the hood, inclined two-cylinder engine under front compartment, driving rear axle by chain, and fuel tank under the driver's seat. There was no differential, but rear springs were mounted outboard for added stability.

The Model 17 seven-passenger Steam Touring Car of 1909 (bottom right) was the last and largest of the Lane steamers. It had a two-cylinder, 30 hp, compound engine, $3\frac{7}{8}$ and $6\frac{1}{4}$x4 in. mounted at 45° under the front floorboards, deriving steam from a semi-flash type boiler, 24 in. in diameter, located under the hood. With "steel frame, Timken roller bearings and automatic fuel and water regulation," price was $3,100—the high in a four-model range. The Lane Motor Vehicle Company, Poughkeepsie, N. Y., had reached the end of its 15-year existence. •

Leach

"WAFFLE" type upholstery and a folding Victoria top were beauty features of this 1900 Leach Motor Carriage, Pattern No. 2. Driven by a two-cylinder, slide-valve, six hp reversible engine of the vertical type, it derived steam from a tubular boiler which could raise 150 psi working pressure in five minutes. With enough water for 35 miles and gas for 100 miles, weight was 700 pounds. "For an operating cost of half a cent per mile," claimed manufacturer, "the Leach will run from one to 40 mph and climb a 14 per cent grade at 15 mph." The engine, "one of the prettiest pieces of mechanism in a motor vehicle," was "noiseless, entirely free from vibration—in fact, simplicity put into steel." Nor was there any "heat or disagreeable odor from boiler or fuel." Pattern No. 2 Motor Carriage, "intended only for good roads," cost from $600 to $800 according to equipment and was one of a three model choice (including a commercial vehicle) with a high of $1,200. The Leach Motor Vehicle Company, Everett, Mass., was another to fall by the wayside within a two-year span—1899-1900. •

Marlboro

GRANDSTAND APPEARANCE of the 1901 Marlboro Model "B" Steam Automobile was typical of contemporary auto body design. This machine had a two-cylinder, horizontal, double-acting engine that produced five hp at 300 rpm. A water-tube boiler with 414 seamless copper tubes tested to 900 psi for safety, built a working steam pressure of 200 psi. The copper water tank held 25 gallons and the gasoline tank 10 gallons. Weight, complete, was 1,050 pounds.

The Marlboro would do 30 mph on "fair roads," 25 mph on "poor roads" and could climb a 25 per cent grade. Built by a concern that had been in the carriage business for 25 years previously, it was the subject of rather cautious advertising. "It is normally unsafe to travel over the road faster than 15 mph, and in building our automobile our aim from the first has been simplicity in every part. With this end in view we studied everything on the market in the way of a carriage and decided on the steam auto being best for all around work for the average person. Gasoline machinery is too complicated and electric vehicles are not practical in the country." The Model "B" at $1,000 was the costliest in a range of three models starting at $750. The Marlboro Automobile and Carriage Company, Marlborough, Mass., produced its first steamer in 1899 and the last in 1902. •

Maryland

AMONG EARLY ATTEMPTS at manufacturing steam commercial vehicles was this Maryland Steam Delivery Wagon of 1901. A two-cylinder, double slide valve, vertical engine, 2½x4½ in. with an output of 12 hp at 2,000 rpm, drove the rear axle by chain through a countershaft. The seamless tubular boiler, tested to 600 psi cold water pressure, had two washout plugs for easy cleaning. It made 180 psi of working steam from a 50-gallon water tank and a 10-gallon gasoline container. Weight of this vehicle was 2,000 pounds, and with a 1,000-pound payload it would do 30 mph and climb a 15 per cent grade. Stated maker: "It can be used in all sections of the country for all purposes, in all kinds of weather on all kinds of roads, with a positive assurance of reaching one's destination without a breakdown." Practical features included watertight, dust-proof roller bearings on all wheels which required oiling only three or four times yearly, and a steam-driven auxiliary boiler feed pump and air compressor, both controlled from the front seat. Equipped with a pilot light, this Delivery Wagon could be left standing "for hours without attention, carrying a full head of steam." There were nine models to choose from with a price range of $900 to $2,500, including a Surrey, Phaeton and Runabout. Incorporated in 1900 with a capital of only $5,000, the Maryland Automobile Manufacturing Company, Luke, Md., stopped building steamers at the close of 1901 when it became the Sinclare-Scott Company, which produced gas powered autos until 1909. •

McDonald

"COME AND GO" was the fate of the 1923 McDonald Steam Bobcat, one of a pair of newcomers in the steam car world that year. Featured was a horizontal, rear mounted two-cylinder slide valve engine, unit-built with the rear axle which it drove by "patented direct drive." A boiler unit under the hood produced superheated steam at some 450 psi, using kerosene fuel; weight was 3,100 pounds. The McDonald Steam Bobcat Roadster was claimed "flexible to a degree never possible in a gas propelled automobile" and would go "from two mph or less to any speed desired." Manufacture does not seem to have progressed much beyond some prototypes, for at this time, Duncan McDonald, founder of the concern, was prepared "after years of experimentation, to start immediately on the production of steam driven automobiles and steam driven power plants . . ." Besides this, early production was to include "converting gas driven cars into steamers." The Bobcat could be obtained either in chassis form or as a complete car, not only in Roadster form but "in all body styles," with prices according to requirements, available on application. Founded in May 1923, the McDonald Steam Automotive Corporation, Garfield, Ohio, vanished from the steam car market a year later. •

Meteor

THE METEOR Steam Tonneau for 1903 was introduced by a firm organized the previous year in succession to the Reading Steam Vehicle Company, which it absorbed. Power was supplied by a four-cylinder, horizontal engine of 10 hp, 3½x4 in., using Stephenson link motion. Steam was built in a vertical water tube boiler with 713 copper tubes, offering 100 sq. ft. of heating surface and a working pressure of 200 psi. Carried were 45 gallons of water and 12 of gas, giving a 1,600 pound weight. Road speed was a "comfortable" 30 mph, and no torch was required to start the burner. Featuring wheel steering, a ratchet-type locking handbrake and a gas tank located under the driver's seat, this steamer was "built along the French gasoline lines, with detachable tonneau seats." Including fenders and lamps, not shown, it sold for $2,000 and was the highest priced of three models starting at $800. The Meteor Engineering Company, Reading, Pa., lasted only two years, closing its door at the turn of 1903, but during that time it continued building the Reading Steam Carriage as a lower-priced companion car. •

Milwaukee

A TYPICAL steam surrey of the period was this 1901 four-passenger Style "H" Steam Vehicle equipped with a two-cylinder, vertical slide-valve engine, 2½x3½ in., which produced five hp at 450 rpm. Drive was by chain from a counter-shaft to the rear axle. The boiler contained 350 copper tubes offering 50 sq. ft. of heating surface. It was tested to 1,000 pounds (cold water) and could produce a working head of 150 psi steam in four minutes from cold. The 30 gallons of water and 10 of gasoline carried were enough for 75 miles with a weight of 1,100 pounds. Gas consumption figured at 12 mpg and speed was up to 30 mph. Among an impressive list of "40 Reasons" why the motorists should buy a Milwaukee Steamer were: seamless boiler; bronze instead of ball bearings for the engine; a crankshaft forged in one piece, "dispensing with the usual 13 to 47 pieces"; a double-acting bronze brake which held "absolutely, forward or backward and cost five times as much as the brake used on any other steam vehicle." Every machine sold was tested on "a severe hillclimb and a 38-mile trip before shipment," while the engine and boiler had been duly tested by the "scientific department of a foremost university." A claim made by a Mr. C. C. Slocum of the Bindley Hardware Co., that his Milwaukee Steamer was the first car to climb Mount Washington, seems to have been a bit optimistic. Several others, led by a Stanley, had been there before him. The Milwaukee Automobile Co., Milwaukee, Wisconsin, offered five models from $750, with the Panel Back Style "H" at $1,300 as the costliest. Equipment included two rubber mats, side lamps and covers, an odometer, a rubber storm apron, a torch (for starting) and all necessary tools. Firm was in business from 1900 to 1902. •

Mobile

"ABSOLUTELY UNEQUALLED on the market today, at any price," was the claim made for the 1900 Model No. 4 Standard Mobile Solid Back steam buggy (shown above), whose manufacturer was hot in competition with his former partner—the Locomobile Company. Powered by a two-cylinder, vertical slide-valve engine of 10 hp, this machine derived a working steam pressure from a fire-tube boiler at 180 psi. Capacity was 22½ gallons of water and 6½ of gasoline; weight, equipped, 700 pounds. An identical model stole the limelight for steam cars at the Madison Square Garden Auto Show in New York with a daily hill-climbing demonstration of goat-like agility. The Mobile regularly climbed and descended a 200 ft. wooden ramp with a 53 ft. rise between the roof and tower of the Garden, providing four different grades between 35 and 42 per cent. Speed on the level was an easy 25 mph and these performances attracted two notable buyers. One was the president of the Brooklyn Street Railway System who used the little steamer for inspecting the electric railway, the other was Colonel John Jacob Astor who drove from his New York offices on countless real estate inspection tours. The Mobile Company of America, Kingsland Point, Tarrytown-on-the-Hudson, N. Y., offered 11 different models between $925 and $1,800, of which the Model No. 4 steam buggy was the least expensive. These machines were sold by 58 agencies and 10 factory branches from coast to coast, yet the firm, founded a year earlier, survived only until the end of 1903.

Of similar specifications was the 1900 Mobile Light Delivery Steam Wagon, Model No. 16 (opposite page, top) except that the water tank held 37 gallons and the gas tank 8¼ gallons. Extra heavy duty Hartford single tube tires were fitted, and the weight was 1,300 pounds. Carrying capacity (exclusive of driver and helper) was 400 pounds; price, $1,350.

Room for six passengers was one of the main attractions of the 1901 Heavy Two-Seated Surrey (opposite page, bottom). Two-cylinder, slide-valve engine, 2½x3½ in., derived working steam from the tubular boiler at 180 psi; water capacity was 25½ gallons and the gas tank held 6¼ gallons. Price, for a weight of 1,450 pounds, was $1,400. No less than 20 different types of

Mobile steamers were offered that year, with a $550 to $2,500 price range.

A 1902 highlight of the Mobile range was the Model No. 13 Long Distance Steam Touring Wagon (see top of page 116) with folding front seat and space for six people. The two-cylinder, slide-valve, vertical engine put out 12 hp and drove the rear axle by conventional chain. Boiler specifications were as formerly, but the water tank held 80 gallons and the gas tank 26¼ gallons. Curb weight was some 1,600 pounds and a steady 35 to 40 mph could be maintained on anything like a road. Model No. 13 had seats 48 in. wide with a solid back rear seat, a 64 in. wheelbase and oversized four-inch Hartford tires for added comfort. The "wire suspension" wheels were 30 in. in diameter. Selling for $1,325, this machine was one of a seven model choice between $1,000 and $2,000.

The prim Model No. 50 Steam Coupe for 1903 (bottom of page 116) was part of the last range of steamers offered by the Mobile Company of America before it went out of business. By then the firm was proudly claiming that it had built 6,000 cars in five years, with "never a single explosion or accident with the boiler." The two-cylinder engine was retained, together with a vertical copper tube boiler that built 180 psi of working steam. Water tank held 72 gallons and fuel tank 16 gallons, but the modified burner now permitted the use either of gasoline or kerosene. Said Mobile: "Ours is the only steam car fully automatic in

The 1900 Mobile Light Delivery Steam Wagon, above, carried 400 pounds plus driver and helper; cost $1,350. Room for six passengers was one of the main attractions of the 1901 Heavy Surrey, below.

A highlight of the 1902 range of models was this Model 13 Long Distance Steam Wagon, above. One of the last offered was the 1903 Model 50, below.

every detail. It is an evolution from the original Whitney and Stanley patents through a million miles of travel experience and half a million dollars of experimental work. Maximum safety is assured because of ease of control."

That year a Mobile Steam Touring Car was driven from Seattle to San Francisco, "the most difficult auto trip on record," which spanned 988¾ miles through places where a two-horse team could not take a wagon. Some of the grades were "so steep that the auto slid down without the wheels moving." Driver was George Carmack, a hardy soul who thrived on adventure and had discovered the Klondike in 1869. No trouble was experienced. Mobile's last appearance featured 15 models, (including a Heavy Truck) from $550 for the Runabout to $3,000 for the Model No. 50 Coupe, rated as a luxury job. The Special Runabout was claimed "the lowest priced auto ever offered to the public by any manufacturer in the country, and the best."

A Mobile Specialty was the Automatic Water Regulator (opposite page, top) used on all 1903 models. Of simple, almost fool-

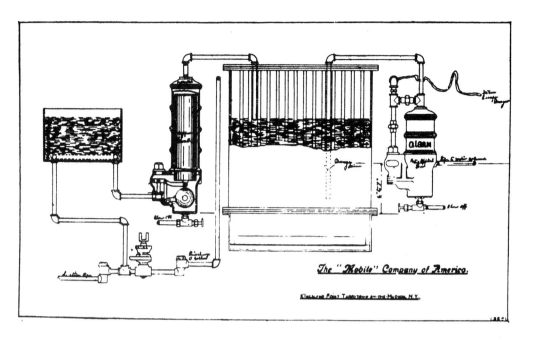

The "Mobile" Company of America.

Kingsland Point, Tarrytown-on-the-Hudson, N.Y.

proof design, its operation depended on the difference in specific gravity between steam and water. With boiler water at the correct level, pressure forced it into the regulator (left, above) causing a balance cup to rise and float. This movement opened a needle valve in the regulator and allowed steam pressure to close the check valve on the left side of the pump, stopping the flow of dater from tank to pumps. When boiler water fell below the mouth of the tube, steam was forced through into the regulator where it pushed down the copper float. The needle valve auto-matically closed, removing steam pressure from pump to check valve and permitting water to be pumped into the boiler.

The Water Indicator, designed to "give notice of low water in the boiler," worked on the same principle.

Main building of the Mobile Company's factory at Kingsland Point, Tarrytown-on-the-Hudson, N. Y., is shown below as it looked in 1903. Adjacent to Philipse Manor Station, it was served by the New York Central and Hudson railroads. Original Stanley Steamer buildings were greatly enlarged after 1899. •

Moncrief

A HAND-BUILT machine of outstandingly good finish was this 1901 Moncrief Steam Wagon, powered by a two-cylinder, link reversing engine of seven hp. It featured an upright water-tube boiler with 70 sq. ft. of heating surface which produced 180 psi of working steam. Water capacity was 35 gallons; gas, 14 gallons, for a weight of 1,700 pounds. Capable of 25 mph, the Moncrief embodied a tubular steel frame of advanced design, chain drive, and wood wheels with solid rubber tires. Priced at $1,000 and manufactured by the James A. Moncrief Company, Pawtucket, R. I., it sold in very limited numbers between 1901 and 1902. •

Morgan

THE THREE-TON 1903 Morgan Power Truck (see opposite page, bottom) was another unsuccessful attempt by a steamer to displace the gasoline vehicle in the commercial field. Motive power came from a large two-cylinder compound engine, 3 and 6x5 in., fed from a "new type" water-tube vertical boiler (right) tested to 600 psi steam pressure and 1,200 cold water pressure. Spaghetti-like maze of 120 tubes made up the boiler of the 1903 Morgan Power Truck. Each tube was welded at the top and pressure-sleeved at the bottom. Burner was located inside this complicated maze. It produced 200 psi of working steam in 20 minutes, from a 100 gallon water tank and two 25 gallon crude oil containers—enough for 100 miles of running. "We are prepared," said maker, "to furnish vehicles with tops to suit the fancy of the purchaser. Price will very cheerfully be estimated upon." The Morgan Steam Truck was tested for at least 100 miles before delivery, after which the final finish varnish was applied. "If pride is naturally felt in a finished Morgan product, we believe it is quite pardonable and fully justified." The Morgan Motor Company, Worcester, Mass., had a brief existence from 1903 to 1904. •

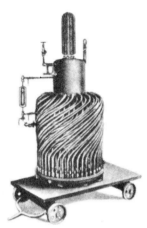

Morse

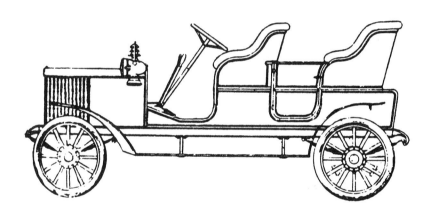

FAR BETTER KNOWN in later years for its line of gasoline cars, the Morse Vehicle Company also built this 1905 Steam Car with a horizontal single-acting engine of 20 hp that had three independent cylinders. Kerosene fuel was used for the flash-type boiler which derived water from a 25 gallon tank. "Special features" included direct drive to the rear axle which had no differential; a burner controlled by automatic steam pressure and a steam throttle on the steering wheel.

Named after Sewall Morse of Detroit who was the "most interested party" in the company and also its president, the Morse steamer first appeared in 1904. The firm was founded in October that year with a capital of $250,000, of which $155,000 was subscribed immediately, showing that interest in steam cars was "still alive." Simultaneously, however, Morse also built a gasoline auto. The steamer survived until 1906 and the internal combustion job until 1909, but that was not the end of the Morse. In March 1910, this firm became the Easton Machine Company, Springfield, Mass., and a new gasoline auto was produced. •

National

ONE OF THE EARLIEST and most ambitious attempts at commercial road transportation was this 1899 National Transportation Steam Bus with an engine "specially constructed by a Dorchester firm." This was a compound, horizontal, two-cylinder job of "10 to 15 hp" deriving steam from a water-tube boiler mounted in front. The water tank held 100 gallons and the fuel tank 40 gallons of kerosene. Weight of this vehicle was 6,000 pounds, equipped with a "thin steel" body 18 ft. long that had a "small amount" of wood paneling.

Incorporated in 1899 under New Jersey laws, the National Transportation Company, Boston, Mass., was started with a capital of $50,000. A contemporary announcement stated: "We have 32 buses under construction, six of which are to be running in the town of Winthrop (Mass.) by June 17; six more to be added soon after. Other routes where street railroads are not wanted have also been secured by the company." The license for public transportation granted the firm by the town of Winthrop ran for a year and stipulated that "the fare shall not exceed five cents (children at half price) and that tires shall not be less than 2½ in. wide." Negotiations also were under way for franchises in Milton and other towns near Boston. The National Steam Bus provided seating for 21 to 40 persons, with the motorman in front "and a small amount of vestibule overhang at the rear." The design obviously was the result of careful thought, but there is no record of this company's survival into 1900. •

Neustadt-Perry

KNOWN as the Steam Combination Car No. 6, this 1902 two- or four-passenger buggy with a folding front seat was only one of a wide range of automotive products manufactured by the Neustadt-Perry Company, St. Louis, Mo. Powered by a two-cylinder, vertical slide valve engine of 10 hp located under the seat, it derived steam from a water-tube boiler which built 160 psi working pressure. Water and gas tanks (rear mounted) held 25 and 10 gallons and final drive was by chain. Weight of this vehicle was 1,000 pounds, with price "according to equipment." If desired, it could be supplied in kit form for home construction. "We supply all parts to complete gasolene or steam vehicles which are the most attractive on the market," claimed the firm. Also in its line was a "gasolene Touring Car." Life span: 1902-1903. •

THIRD OF A TRIO of steam buggies manufactured in the small town of Waltham, Mass., the New England Steam Carriage of 1899 featured a two-cylinder, vertical, "high-pressure engine set on the quarter so that dead center is overcome." The fire-tube boiler, tested to 750 psi, produced 160 psi of working steam and had a safety valve set to blow-off at 200 pounds. Enough water was carried for 35 to 40 miles, and sufficient gasoline for 200 miles, fed to the burner by air pressure at 10 to 15 pounds. Weighing 600 pounds, this buggy could be run "at any speed required, with 10 to 15 mph a good average." Braking was the firm's particular pride. "The carriage can be stopped in six feet from 10 to 12 mph. The brake lever is in a convenient position so that the foot rests on it all the time." The New England Motor Carriage Company set the delivery of its first production models for June 1899, but the manufactured life of this "very graceful carriage" ended in 1900. •

New York

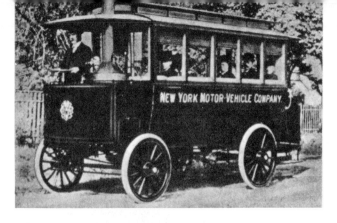

A PUBLIC TRANSIT VEHICLE that actually went into operation at the turn of the century was this 1900 New York Steam Bus, driven from New York to Buffalo for exhibition at the Pan American Exposition. Power unit was a two-cylinder, horizontal, compound engine, 4 and 7x5 in., driving the rear axle by chains through a countershaft. Steam was derived from a vertical Morrin Climax boiler of a type used on stationary engines. Mounted in front, it consisted of 200 copper tubes tested to 600 psi cold water pressure. The burner, "of the French Longuemare type," was supplied from a 15-gallon kerosene tank and an 80-gallon container of water. Built in one model which weighed 3¼ tons, this commercial steamer did 12 mph at 500 rpm and was designed to carry 20 passengers. The chassis, built by F. R. Wood & Son, had a wheelbase of 9½ ft. and a tread of 7 ft. It ran on wood wheels with solid rubber tires. Wood alcohol was used as a primer to start the heating, and the company declared itself to be working on an "improved balanced engine capable of an unusually high speed." Founded in 1900, the company remained in business for one year. •

Porter

NAMED AFTER Major D. Porter, "a pioneer in motor manufacture since 1886," the 1900 Porter Steam Stanhope used an engine adopted by very few steam vehicle builders. This was a two-cylinder, single-acting, oscillating type, "balanced throughout," and steam-fed from a tubular boiler which contained 350 copper tubes tested to 1,000 pounds cold water pressure. Working steam was at 150 psi from a water and kerosene (or gasoline) supply adequate for 50 miles. Dry weight was 550 pounds and running costs worked out a half a cent per mile at 15 mph "over ordinary roads." Maximum speed was around 25 mph. Aluminum-built, the body featured watertight compartments making the Porter "the only perfect automobile that has no rival in simplicity, design, construction and economy." The low-draft burner is unquenchable in all weathers, and one of the noteworthy features of the Porter vehicle is that it cannot become unmanageable. Controlled by a single lever, power is shut off the minute the hand is removed, and the vehicle stops. Neither odor, noise nor vibration can be noticed." In those days, Eastern Massachusetts was generally considered the home of the steam vehicle, and the Porter Motor Company, Boston, Massachusetts, was located right in the heart of this territory where it had a factory "100x36 ft." with "the latest machinery and equipment for manufacturing." The Porter steamer managed to survive only from 1900 to 1901. •

Prescott

"GETS THERE AND BACK," was the tag applied to the Model No. 1 Prescott Steam Automobile introduced in 1901. The two-cylinder, vertical engine, mounted under the driving seat, was of 7¼ hp with plain bearings and drove the rear axle by chain. Steam came from a super-heater boiler with 364 copper tubes, tested to 700 psi cold water and producing 200 psi of working pressure. With 32 gallons of water and a filled 12-gallon gasoline tank of seamless copper, weight was 1,050 pounds. Performance was apparent in the Speed Trials held on Staten Island Boulevard, May 31, 1902, when a stock Prescott covered a mile in one minute, 37⅕ seconds, "proving conclusively that Prescotts are safe, speedy and reliable." Another of these steamers was awarded a first class certificate in the Automobile Club of America's 100-Mile Endurance Contest from New York to Southport, held on Decoration Day. Customer had the choice of black finish with royal blue panels, or dark brewster green with cardinal red panels. Running gear was green or red, to suit, and patent leather fenders were available as an extra. Manufacturer called his product "a perfect two-passenger carriage with graceful, artistic lines, that will carry four." Model No. 1 shown with extra seat open, sold for $1,000 complete and was the lowest-priced of four models with a $1,250 high. The Prescott Automobile Manufacturing Company, Passiac, New Jersey, flourished from 1901 through 1905. •

Puritan

WHEEL STEERING with a jointed pillar that allowed the wheel to be "folded over and out of the way while mounting or dismounting," was an unusual feature of this Puritan 1902 Steam Car. A two-cylinder, vertical, six hp engine was used, and the fire-tube boiler built 180 psi of working steam pressure derived from a 32-gallon water tank and a 16-gallon gas tank. Weight was 1,000 pounds; claimed speed 20 mph "easily maintained with four passengers." A new feature claimed by the firm was a "foot controlled throttle in place of the usual hand lever." The pilot light on the burner enabled a full head of steam to be maintained for long periods when the machine was not in use, but because of fire risks and boosted insurance premiums, most garages refused to accept steamers unless the pilot light was extinguished. Rakishly swept front fenders on this little steamer were just coming into fashion. Builders were the Locke Regulator Company, Salem, Mass.; 1901 to 1904. •

Reading

STRENGTH, reliability and smooth running were the virtues claimed for this Model "C" Reading Steam Carriage, 1901 vintage. The vertical engine was a four-cylinder job of 5¾ hp, and the tubular boiler tested to 700 psi offered 60 sq. ft. of heating surface. Working steam pressure of 140 to 180 psi could be raised from cold in less than 10 minutes. Water tank held 32 gallons (enough for 30 miles) against eight of gasoline which were good for up to nine hours of running, depending on the speed. This steamer could propel its 1,000-pound weight at an average of 15 mph and had a maximum of 30 mph. It was described as "a strong, practical machine which can be safely operated and will withstand the wear and tear of the most arduous work to which a road wagon can be subjected." Starting was by means of an auxiliary vaporizer in which a little alcohol was poured and ignited, and the machine was claimed to have "none of the throbbing and shaking that accompanies the operation of the ordinary automobile." At $850, Model "C" was the lowest priced of a range offering three types with a high of $1,000. Founded in 1900, the Steam Vehicle Company of America had its factory in Reading, Pa., and also Stables at 160 West 56th Street, New York City. It was absorbed in 1902 by the Meteor Engineering Company, who introduced a larger model but continued producing the Reading Steam Carriage until 1903.

The 1901 Reading twin-cylinder steam engine (right) featured a roller-bearing crankshaft, rotary valves and an aluminum jacket filled with asbestos lagging for improved heat insulation. Cylinders were 2½x3½ in. •

Richmond

PRETTY MUCH STANDARD in specifications was this 1903 Richmond Steam Runabout with a Dos-a-Dos body seating four when front seat was opened. It had a two-cylinder, vertical slide engine of six hp and a 16-in. fire-tube boiler by Kelly which produced 160 psi of working steam. Carried were 25 gallons of water and 12 of gasoline for weight of 1,400 pounds. The front seat was 36x20 in.; rear seat 34x20 in. A burner of Kelly manufacture supplied the heat, and the body was hinged at the rear, "making parts easily accessible." The Richmond Automobile and Cycle Company, Richmond, Indiana, began building steam cars in 1902 and stopped about a year later. •

Rochester

THE 1901 Steam Runabout shown in the top photo was made "to fill the demand for a high grade mechanical vehicle combining the very best quality workmanship and material with Simplicity, Practicability and Durability." The vertical, two-cylinder, four hp engine was "capable of a 75 per cent overload," and secured steam from a seamless tubular boiler made up of copper tubes tested to 600 psi cold water pressure and 400 psi steam. Enough water (35 gallons) was carried for a 35-mile trip; and six gallons of gas were good for about 70 miles. On a dollar per pound basis the Rochester—$750 for 900 pounds weight— was good value, but it had other claims to excellence. "The engine is the life of the automobile," stated maker, "and the Rochester engine is perfect." Equipment included a pilot light for immediate starting and a double French-plate hinged mirror to show the water gauge day and night. In common with so many other steam car builders, the life of the Rochester Cycle Manufacturing Company, Rochester, N. Y., was a woefully brief one. It began in 1900 and ended in 1901.

The swivel-type tubular frame of the car (above) was unusually flexible. Groping toward "independent" suspension, it allowed either front wheel 15 inches of up-and-down movement as shown by wooden block, with no appreciable disturbance of body level. •

Ross

THE LONG HOOD of this 1906 Ross Steam Touring Car, adorned with a large false radiator "which adds to the attractive appearance," housed both engine and boiler. Power unit was a two-cylinder, vertical, 25 hp job with Stephenson valve gear, and the boiler bed was riveted to the frame. Steam at a working pressure of 375 psi was raised from a 45-gallon copper water tank with six compartments and a 25-gallon pressed steel gasoline container. Shipping weight of this steamer was 2,600 pounds for a "comfortable" performance of 35 to 45 mph. Features included shaft drive and starting by Bunsen burner fed from an auxiliary acetylene tank which ignited "instantly with a match." One model was offered with two sets of brakes and a double entrance wooden body at a price of $2,800. In 1908 a Runabout was added with a $2,250 tag. Manufacturer Louis S. Ross of Newtonville, Mass., launched his steamer in 1905 and continued production until 1909. Five-year span was unusually long. •

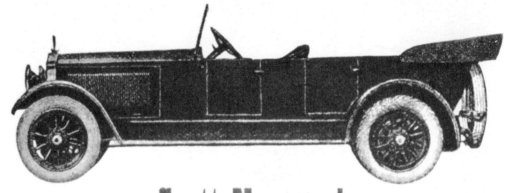

Scott-Newcomb

THIS INTERESTING new Steam Touring Car hit the market in May 1921, carrying with it the work and hopes of three prominent engineers in the field of steam development. Name was derived from two of its mentors—designer L. L. Scott, assisted by Dr. E. C. Newcomb, who jointly had spent three years developing their steamer. Third on the team was Professor A. C. Staley, associate professor of automotive design at Purdue University, Lafayette, Indiana, at one time connected with the development of the Stanley and Doble Detroit Steam Cars, and later associated with the Coats Steam Car Company. Outcome of this brain trust was a machine far above average in design. The engine was a two-cylinder, horizontal, double-acting job of 40 hp with cylinders 4x5 in., unit-built with rear axle which it drove direct. The water-tube flash-type boiler offered 72 sq. ft. of heating surface and could raise 600 psi of working steam in one minute. The water tank held 25 gallons—enough for 150 to 350 miles, according to speed and conditions; choice of fuel included kerosene, gasoline, gas oil, fuel oil or a mixture of any of these in any proportions. No lightweight, the Scott-Newcomb scaled 4,200 pounds at the curb, but it would do 60 mph with ease and could run 12 to 15 mpg on kerosene with a seven-passenger load.

Starting procedure was as follows: "Car is stone cold. Switch on the dash is turned and the electric motor starts the water and paraffin pumps. A continuous spark at the plug points starts the burner flame and in one minute a head of steam sufficient to get away is available. After two seconds the plug stops sparking and the control of water and fire is then entirely automatic. When the car is running at 25 mph on a level road, the motor will be working for about one-third of the

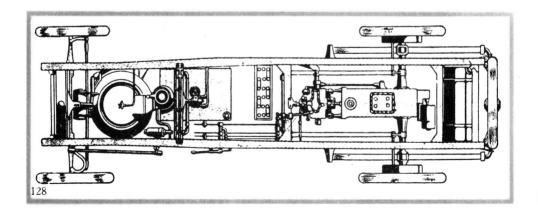

total time." To reduce unsprung weight, the engine of the Scott-Newcomb was carried half on the frame and half on the rear axle, and over-all weight distribution was very good. So promising were the first cars produced under the auspices of the Standard Engineering Company, St. Louis, Mo., that in July 1921, the firm announced a projected Standard Steam Truck of 2 or 2½ tons capacity was under way and deliveries would begin in June 1922, with an expected production schedule of 2,000 vehicles. As a result, the Fifth Avenue Coach Company, New York, investigated the Scott-Newcomb with a view to inaugurating steamers on their system, but apparently nothing came of this. Price of the passenger car was not determined as it was not at this time "available in quantities on the market," but if ever a steamer got off to a good start it was this one. Yet, with the passing of another year, nothing more was heard of it.

Carefully balanced layout of chassis components resulted in excellent weight distribution (see opposite page, bottom). Between rear gas tank and axle was the electric generator driven through extension gearing. Unit-built engine was flexibly mounted to allow for up-and-down movement of rear axle which carried one end of it. Battery was slung amidships, followed by water tank (with fuel and water pumps above it), then by boiler, low in the frame and well behind the front axle.

Neatly tucked under hood, continuous flow flash-type boiler was started by the turn of a switch. Waste steam powered the condenser cooling fan, not shown here. So efficient was the boiler that the car would run a mile on the steam in the tubes, after the fire was shut off. •

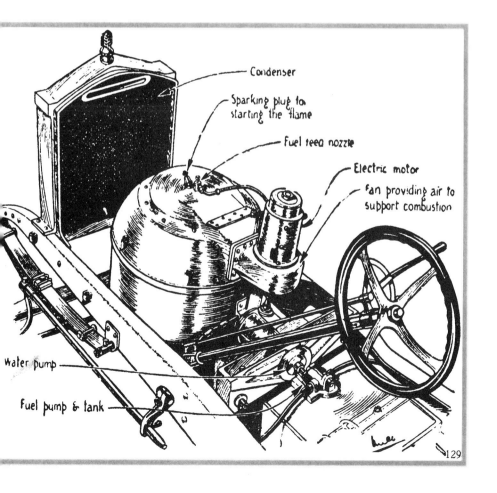

Condenser

Sparking plug for starting the flame

Fuel feed nozzle

Electric motor

Fan providing air to support combustion

Water pump

Fuel pump & tank

129

Skene

EVERY PART of this 1900 light steam buggy "except the tires" was made on the spot at the factory of the J. W. Skene Cycle & Automobile Co., Lewiston, Maine. This was unusual in a day when countless assembled steamers mushroomed briefly, bringing temporary prosperity to all kinds of component manufacturers. The Skene Steam Carriage had a two-cylinder, upright five hp engine powered by a water-tube boiler made up from 350 copper tubes tested to 1,000 psi cold water. Three minutes after applying a match to the burner, 100 psi of steam could be raised, and working pressure of 160 psi was built in four minutes. Enough water for 25 miles and five gallons of gas were carried; weight was 575 pounds and speed up to 50 mph, "limited only by the operator's courage." Safe cruising was at 30 mph with an operational cost of one-fifth of a cent per mile on ordinary roads and one-tenth of a cent on "first class" roads. The Skene would also climb "any grade" where it could get a grip. Evolved from a test car that had run 5,000 miles, the Skene had a "finely finished body to which a canopy top may easily be added." Two models were offered on the same chassis: a single-seater at $1,000 and the two-seater Stanhope for $1,250. Firm's manufacturing span was 1900 through 1901. ●

Steamobile

CUTENESS was tenor of ads extolling this 1900 Style "A" Steamobile Buggy (top photo) as "Just one Little Wagon made by One Little Factory in One Little New Hampshire Town—but in simplicity and efficiency The Biggest Thing on wheels." A vertical, double-acting, two-cylinder engine, 3x3½ in., developed seven to nine hp at 100 rpm, driving the rear axle by chain. The water-tube boiler with 420 copper tubes tested to 700 psi steam, offered 52 sq. ft. of heating area and could raise 160 psi of working steam in four minutes. Carried were 25 gallons of water and 8½ of gasoline—"enough for 100 miles on ordinary roads." Weight was 1,220 pounds. In the same vein, maker coyly remarked: "It may not be true, but it is claimed that the Steamobile possesses every improvement and device found on any other steam vehicle, and in addition thereto, 20 essential improvements." The Style "A" steamer, priced at $850 "with full leather top," was one of five models with a low of $750 and a high of $1,100, carrying this reminder: "The *intelligent* buyer studies *quality*, not first cost . . ." Builders, the Keene Automobile Company, Keene, N. H., founded 1900, became the Steamobile Company of America in 1902 and folded in 1904.

The 1901 Dos-a-Dos buggy (above), built on a flexible tubular swivel-type frame, featured same specifications as previous year but carried 26 gallons of water and eight of gasoline. Equipped to seat four, it weighed 1,306 pounds and brought $1,300, being the highest priced model that year. Finish was in black and brewster green and the equipment included syphons, water raiser, a canvas bucket, extra chain links and an odometer. Optional extras were a touring hamper, $20, Midgley tubular steel wheels enameled to match for $30, long distance tires by the Belting and Packing Company at $40, f.o.b. Keene, N. H. •

Stearns

CONFIDENTIALLY ALOOF in the Steam versus Gasoline con- troversy, makers of this 1901 Model "D" Stearns Steam Buggy remarked: "It is not our purpose to enter at this time into an argument as to the relative merit of the different kinds of power used to propel vehicles. Steam, the principles of which are taught in our schools, its universal use in our factories, for marine propulsion and on our great railroads, is, we believe, the best power for driving automobiles." The Model "D" car had a two-cylinder, slide-valve, vertical engine and a tubular boiler of conventional design which produced 160 psi of working steam "very quickly." Sufficient water for 35 miles and gasoline for 50 miles were carried, resulting in a weight of 875 pounds. Performance of this steamer was demonstrated in the New York to Rochester Endurance Contest, run September 9 to 13, 1901, when a Stearns covered 394.3 miles in 32 hours, 21 minutes, at an average of 12.2 mph. This machine also scooped a second prize in the Nelson Hillclimb, wending up 2,372 ft. in 4 minutes, 2 seconds. Finished in olive and bottle green striped with carmine, and equipped with a top

of the "finest hand buffed leather, including side curtains," Model "D" brought $875. It was one of seven models with a range of $800 to $1,200. The Stearns Steam Carriage Company, Syracuse, N. Y., lasted from 1900 through 1903.

Probably the forerunner of all production Station Wagons was the 1902 Stearns Model "H" Station Wagon (shown above) with roll-down canvas sides. Its two-cylinder, double-acting engine, $2\frac{1}{2}$x$3\frac{1}{2}$ in. was of eight hp, and the 16-in. boiler remained unchanged. Water tank held 22 gallons, gas tank, eight gallons, weight 1,100 pounds. Mounted on an $81\frac{1}{4}$-in. wheelbase chassis, with 28-in. wire wheels and 3-in. pneumatic tires, the body seated six comfortably, though front passengers had no forward weather protection. Said to "Ride like a Pullman," Model "H" was equipped with "forced boiler draft, new sight-feed cylinder lubricator and sufficient fuel and water for a 100-mile run." The flow of oil from the tank burner was automatically cut off by a thermostat, and the "double-action handbrake" featured a lock. Of nine models produced that year, starting at $900, the Steam Station Wagon for $1,600 was the costliest. •

Sterling

THE 1901 Sterling Steam Carriage (top photo) was a serious attempt to produce something a little different in design from the common run of steam buggies. A two-cylinder, 90° V-type engine of 4½ hp was used in conjunction with a water-tube boiler of the Babcock and Wilcox stationary type, featuring a steam drum and super-heating tubes tested to 400 psi steam. Cold water to 20 psi steam took two minutes and the normal working pressure of 140 psi was attained in five minutes. Carried were 25 gallons of water (30 miles) and five of gasoline (50 miles). Weight was 1,100 pounds, resulting in a 30 mph maximum speed and the ability to climb 40 per cent grades. "We manufacture our own boilers and engines," said the maker, "and our wagons will travel on any ordinary road and will run on muddy roads with reasonable success. Running costs with common gasolene are from one-half to one cent per mile." Price of lone model offered was $750, but in spite of originality the Empire Manufacturing Company, Sterling, Ill., built steamers only from 1901 through 1902.

Interesting chassis of 1901 Sterling Steam Carriage (above) was constructed of "100 per cent steel" with a rigid frame and sub-frame. The rear-mounted V-type engine, 2½x3½ in., drove the right rear wheel direct by spur gear; horizontal boiler was located crosswise. •

Sunset

PRODUCT OF CALIFORNIA was this 1901 Sunset Steam Runabout with a two-cylinder, vertical, slide-valve engine, 2½x3½ in., featuring link reverse action. A 14-in. water-tube boiler produced 150 psi of working steam, supplied by 19 gallons of water and three of gasoline. Dry weight was 450 pounds and "cruising speed" 20 mph. One model, priced at $900 was offered with an exhaust heater and the choice of side or center steering. Formed 1901, the Sunset Auto Co., San Francisco, Calif., built steamers until 1904, then switched to gasoline autos. •

Sweany

AMBITIOUS was this 1895 Sweany Steam Carriage with design ideas far ahead of its time and distinctly beyond practical contemporary workmanship. Each wheel was driven direct by a separate single-cylinder engine of 2½ to 3 hp, deriving steam from a front-mounted water-tube boiler packed with magnesium to prevent heat radiation and neatly encased in patent leather. Steam pressure at 150 psi was supplied by water and "gasolene" tanks located under the front seat, and road weight was 1,350 pounds. De-signed to carry six passengers, the Sweany did 16 to 20 mph (maximum). The engines, which could be run "independently of each other, if desired," were "very small and light—a patented invention giving the greatest amount of power for the size." An ingenious footbrake simultaneously shut off steam as it acted on the wheels and the whole machine presented "a very neat appearance." Unfortunately, it was an experimental job and the Charles S. Caffrey Co., Camden, N. J., never reached production owing to technical bugs. •

Toledo

THE TOLEDO Model "B" Steam Carriage, introduced in 1901 (pictured above) was a beautiful engineering job manufactured by a firm with an iron will to survive at all costs. Power unit was a two-cylinder, horizontal, double-acting job of 6¼ hp. The tubular boiler, tested to 800 psi steam, built 180 psi normal running. Water was contained in a 31-gallon copper tank, giving a range of 35 miles; "gasolene" in two 4½ gallon tanks sufficed for 85 miles. Heavier than usual, this machine scaled 1,500 pounds but had tremendous endurance. On October 14, 1901, a stock Model "B" steamer (with top) set off from Toledo for New York, a distance of 900 miles, carrying two passengers (400 pounds) and 200 pounds of luggage. The crew consisted of George Soules and James S. Mitchell, a 250 pound heavyweight, yet the only spare carried was one inner tube. Roads were "horrible" and the weather "appalling, with frequent snow." For 14 days the steamer battled on, putting in eight to 10½ hours daily and covering from 37 to 78 miles. It reached New York without a breakdown,

setting up "a record without parallel for steam vehicle tests." Every Toledo steamer was given a 50-mile test before delivery, and the copper air tank which fed fuel under pressure to the burner was tested to 200 psi. Model "B," selling for $1,000 was one of four models with an $800 to $1,600 range. Accessories included oil lamps, bell, cyclometer, tools and a throttle lock.

In 1902, when the Model "C" Steam Carriage (top of opposite page) appeared, the American Bicycle Company, Toledo, Ohio, changed its name to the International Motor Car Company, and began making the Toledo Gasoline Touring Car and the Waverly Electric Vehicle in addition to steamers. Betting across the board, the firm was ready to supply the public with any means of locomotion it wanted—a policy that paid off. Model "C" had a two-cylinder, horizontal, slide valve engine of 6¼ hp with cylinders 3x4 in. Steam was built in a water-tube boiler of superheating type, tested to 600 psi cold water and 1,200 psi of steam. The burner featured a pilot light and the working pressure was 175 psi

The 1902 Model "C" Toledo Steam Carriage, above, was the costliest of five models offered at $1,600. The horizontal twin-cylinder engine of the 1901 Toledo, below, had bore and stroke of 3x4., used piston valves.

supplied from 56 gallons of water and nine of gas in a pair of 4½ gallon tanks. Curb weight was 1,700 pounds. The plant, located in five acres of grounds, comprised 449,000 sq. ft. of factory space and the firm was ready for anything. "The automobile movement has probably attracted the attention of the general public to a greater extent than has any other sport or industry. Nothing is more sincerely solicited by the International Motor Car Company than a thorough investigation of its manufacturing methods." Of five models offered that year with a low of $600, the Model "C" Steam Carriage at $1,600 was the costliest. In 1903, seeing the writing on the wall, the company dropped steamer production and concentrated on gasoline autos.

The horizontal twin-cylinder engine of the 1901 Toledo steamer (right) had a bore and stroke of 3x4 in. and used piston valves. Clean design provided neat, compact casings leaving no vital part exposed to dust or dirt. A sprocket on the crank journal drove the rear axle by chain. •

Tractobile

A NOVEL CONCEPT in steam automotive power was the 1901 front-drive Tractobile Tracto-Surrey which could be supplied either as a complete vehicle or as an auxiliary unit that would fit any horse-drawn carriage. The engine was a marvelously compact job consisting of two separate vertical cylinders, each cranking one of the front wheels direct, with the road wheel acting as a flywheel. Equally compact was the fire-tube boiler made up of five separate units, each with 40 small tubes. The complete boiler, including an outer case of "non-conducting material" measured only 27x6 in. There were no rivets and the boiler could be "opened, inspected and cleaned in five minutes." Kerosene or "gasolene" served equally well for fuel, the generated steam supplying "plenty of reserve power for heavy gradients and exceptional occasions." On ordinary roads, a "very smooth gliding action" was secured and the motor exerted "only a small proportion of its power." The boiler units were coupled in series, like a battery, and any of them could be quickly detached. Each was designed to withstand "enormous pressures." Subject of "numerous patents," the Tractobile Steam Attachment (complete with engines, boiler, burner, tanks, forked frame and wheels with pneumatic tires), sold for $450. The firm preferred not to build complete vehicles but to supply the Tractobile to carriage makers. However, for those who preferred everything in one package, the Tracto-Surrey cost $650. There was also a Stanhope at $500 and a Station Wagon for Six which brought $850. The Pennsylvania Steam Vehicle Co., Inc., Carlisle, Pa., founded in 1900 and "composed of prominent men with ample capital," still failed to make the grade, surviving only through 1902. •

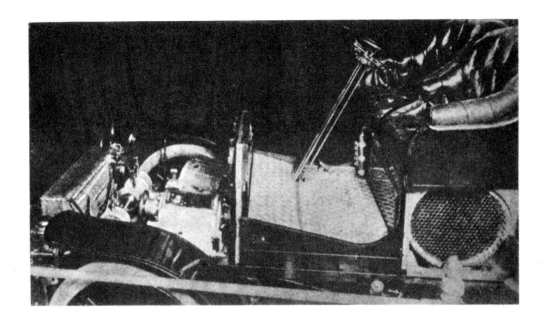

Twombly

The three-section aluminum kerosene burner of the 1904 Twombly Steam Car was of a new design and of ample efficiency. Car could go 25 mph with only two burner surfaces lit, 50 with three.

INTRODUCED in 1904, the Twombly Steam Car was no paragon of beauty but it did feature several original ideas. The engine was a four-cylinder, 12 hp, opposed job of compound type, with two cylinders 3¼x4½ in. and the other two 3¼x5 in. At will it could instantly be converted into a 28 hp single acting type. Shelby seamless tubing was used in the flash-type fire-tube boiler which built 250 psi of working steam pressure and produced 18 hp in an evaporation test. The water tank held 18 gallons —enough for 150 miles, and 12 gallons of gasoline or kerosene were carried for a weight of 1,800 pounds. Both boiler and burner were said to be the first of this type applied to an automobile, and the car could "safely be left for 24 hours to maintain a head of steam after the fire has been lit." Speed was 50 mph "on level roads," with enough power to "sustain a weight up to 4,000 pounds." There were "many unique features" in the two models offered with a price range of $2,500 to $3,000—the one here shown being the lower priced. The Twombly Motor Carriage Company, New York, N. Y., lasted only two years. It closed down after 1905.

The three-section aluminum kerosene burner of the 1904 model was of new design and ample efficiency (left). Two sections of the burner surface were sufficient to maintain a speed of 25 mph. Once lit, it required no attention for 24 hours. •

Victor

AS A SPECIAL INDUCEMENT to customers, this Victor Steam Automobile of 1900 was "insurable and inspectable by the Hartford Inspection and Insurance Company," at a time when steamers were anything but a good insurance risk. The fact that "every part of the carriage is metal, except the seat and floorboards," may have had something to do with this. The Victor had a two-cylinder, vertical engine of four hp "enclosed in an aluminum box." A seamless steel water tube boiler with 425 steel tube flues produced working steam at 150 psi in 10 minutes. A copper water tank held 15 gallons and five gallons of "gasolene fuel" were carried. Weight was 800 pounds. Up to 60 miles could be covered on "ordinary roads" at one filling. An interesting feature was a dual purpose air pressure pump which not only supplied fuel to the burner at 150 psi, but could also be used to inflate the tires.

Described as "an automobile entirely automatic in feeding fuel and water," this buggy had a fusible plug to safeguard the boiler. "Should water fail, the fusible plug melts and automatically shuts off the fuel." One model only was offered. As seen here it cost $850, or with top and full equipment, $950. The Overman Auto Company, Chicopee Falls, Mass., opened its doors in 1899 and built steamers

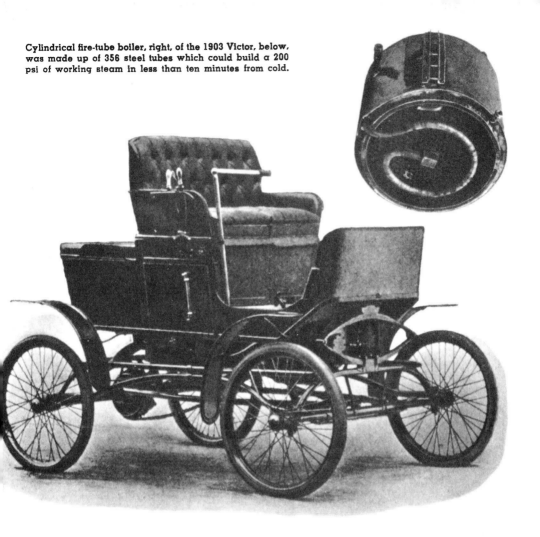

Cylindrical fire-tube boiler, right, of the 1903 Victor, below, was made up of 356 steel tubes which could build a 200 psi of working steam in less than ten minutes from cold.

through 1904. Subsequently it began producing a "Hand Forged Auto Buggy with a two-cycle gas engine."

Getting huskier was the 1903 model of the Victor Steam Carriage (above), with a two-cylinder, piston valve, vertical engine of 4 hp, with cylinders 2½x3 in. The seamless boiler now had 356 steel tubes offering 54 sq. ft. of heating surface and tested to 60° psi cold water pressure. Working steam was stepped up to 200 psi and 27 gallons of water (enough for 22 to 25 miles) were carried. With two five-gallon gas tanks the weight was 1,150 pounds, and the speed 25 to 30 mph over good roads. "Underneath the cushion of the driver's seat," said the maker, "is a spring catch which automatically locks the throttle when the weight of the driver is removed from the seat. This prevents the carriage being started through carelessness or mischief on the part of the passer-by, when the carriage is standing unoccupied." Final drive was by chain and the "standard color" black enamel with red running gear and a red strip around the panels. At $1,200, this buggy was the lower priced of two models with a $1,400 high.

Cylindrical fire-tube boiler (top right) of the 1903 Victor was made up from 356 steel tubes which could build 200 psi of working steam in less than 10 minutes, starting from cold. •

Westfield

MANUFACTURED by one of several firms working both sides of the street at once, this Model "A" 1903 Westfield Steam Runabout was one of several products in a varied automotive line. It had a two-cylinder, slide valve engine of six hp located under the seat, and a "fully enclosed" 16-in. water-tube boiler which produced working steam at 160 psi. Carried were 30 gallons of water and 12 of gasoline, for a weight of 1,250 pounds. The C. G. Moore Manufacturing Co., Westfield, Mass., from which town the car derived its name, made running gear and bodies suitable for either gasoline or steam power. "We are in a position to furnish complete autos ready for power, entirely finished including painting, upholstery, brakes and special motor hangings, and with tires if necessary. We are also in a position to furnish any of our models in part or complete, finished or unfinished." A versatile range of 10 models on three different chassis was available, with prices according to requirements, but even this did not save the firm whose brief span was 1902-1903. •

G. E. Whitney

"CHIEFLY INTERESTED PARTY" in the manufacture of this 1897 Fully Automatic Steam Wagon was a Boston lawyer named George B. Upham who was also mentioned in connection with a Massachusetts motor bill favoring the horseless carriage. Design featured a two-cylinder, slide valve engine and a fully automatic vertical water-tube boiler which produced 100 psi of working steam. Carried were 12 gallons of water and five of "gasolene" for a weight of 650 pounds. Designer and builder George E. Whitney, East Boston, Mass., (at tiller) ascended a 20 per cent grade "without difficulty," and "recently traveled over highways from Boston to Hartford in 10½ hours, a distance registered on the cyclometer of over 130 miles." The Stanley brothers once again began manufacturing steamers in 1900, licensed under George E. Whitney patents. •

R. S. Whitney

TRULY A CUSTOM JOB was this 1905 Whitney Steam Car of similar name but different origin, sold to a Mr. H. J. Potter of Rockland, Maine. Designer R. S. Whitney produced only three steamers bearing his name, of which this one was the last. It had a two-cylinder, horizontal, copper encased engine of eight hp with ballbearing crankshaft and a bore and stroke of 2 5/15x4 in. The tubular boiler, mounted in front, was made from seamless steel and copper tubes to sustain a working pressure of 175 psi. With water tank under the seat and a rear-mounted gas tank, weight was 1,300 pounds. "Perfect control and quiet running" as speeds up to 30 mph were claimed as "special points of excellence." Also, "any part of the car can easily be replaced in case of a breakdown and long delays are avoided." The engine was under the floorboards, driving the rear axle by roller chain, while the all-steel body of $\frac{1}{16}$-in. plates, unit-built with the chassis, not only was "practically indestructible" but probably heralded the first integral body and frame construction ever attempted in this country. To "prevent chafing," the gas tank was enclosed in a wooden box. Not more than one pint of gasoline was "under pressure at any time," seemingly reducing fire and explosion hazards. Mounted on 30-in. wood wheels that had riveted spokes to guard against cracking, this steamer used 3-in. Fisk tires. Price was $1,200.

The first Whitney was completed in 1899 at the Whitney Machine Co.'s Brunswick, Maine, plant. The second appeared in 1902. After 1905, R. S. Whitney transferred his manufacturing facilities to Auburn, Maine, where he produced only automotive repair equipment. •

Wood

THOUGH SOMEWHAT BACKWARD in appearance, the 1903 Wood Vapor Vehicle featured some progressive ideas in steamer design. It was powered by a three-cylinder, eight hp, slide-valve engine which derived steam from "a generator of special design that hangs under the carriage." This was a water-tube, horizontal boiler fired with kerosene and producing a working pressure of 160 psi steam.

Unusually light, this buggy scaled 450 pounds, of which only 80 pounds was taken up by "machinery." Other features were a steam condenser, but "no fire box or smoke stack"; 36-in. wood wheels on solid rubber tires and a bevel gear chainless drive. At $450 this machine, built by the Wood Vapor Vehicle Co., Brooklyn, N. Y., cost exactly a dollar per pound. Its existence was brief: 1902-1903. •

Wood-Loco

UNRELATED was the 1901 Wood-Loco Steam Vehicle here seen in two stages of manufacture. This one had a two-cylinder, horizontal engine of eight hp and a water-tube boiler that built 160 psi working pressure. Water tank held 25 gallons and enough "gasolene or kerosene" was carried for a 60-mile trip. Weight of buggy at left, "built to hold five-passengers" was 900 pounds. Featured were a burner of "special design, allowing perfect combustion"; shaft drive to the rear wheels, and the back portion of the seat opening outward so that the passengers could face each other. Just how the steering problem was overcome under these

conditions was not stated, but the machine was claimed "absolutely safe in the hands of the novice." At this time, Mr. J. C. Wood, president and general manager of the Wood-Loco Vehicle Co., Cohoes, N. Y., (seen with cars) announced his company was "about ready to offer its steam vehicles to the trade." Scheduled for production besides the buggy were two other models of more ambitious type. One was a 1,600-pound Delivery Wagon with a carrying capacity of 3,000 pounds; the other a 10-passenger Commercial Vehicle with a 1,500-pound payload. Nothing much seemed to happen to any of these projects, and by the end of 1902 the firm fizzled out. •